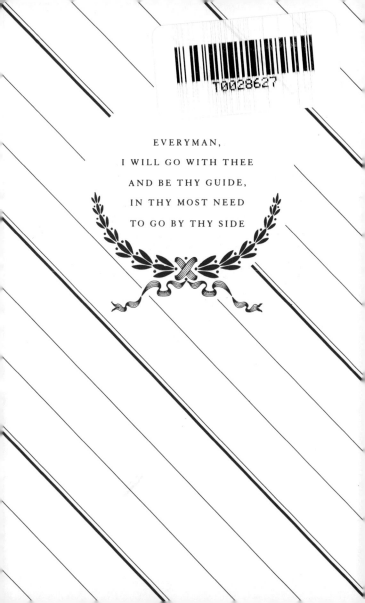

EVERYMAN,
I WILL GO WITH THEE
AND BE THY GUIDE,
IN THY MOST NEED
TO GO BY THY SIDE

EVERYMAN'S LIBRARY
POCKET POETS

POEMS
OF
PARIS

••••••••••••••••••••

EDITED BY
EMILY FRAGOS

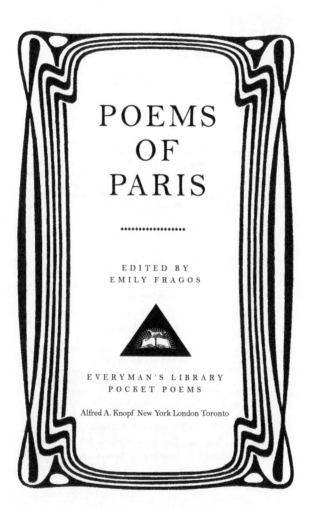

EVERYMAN'S LIBRARY
POCKET POEMS

Alfred A. Knopf New York London Toronto

THIS IS A BORZOI BOOK
PUBLISHED BY ALFRED A. KNOPF

This selection by Emily Fragos first published in
Everyman's Library, 2019
Copyright © 2019 by Everyman's Library

Fourth printing (US)

A list of acknowledgments to copyright owners appears at the back
of this volume.

All rights reserved. Published in the United States by Alfred A. Knopf, a
division of Penguin Random House LLC, New York, and in Canada by
Penguin Random House Canada Limited, Toronto. Distributed by Penguin
Random House LLC, New York. Published in the United Kingdom by
Everyman's Library, 50 Albemarle Street, London W1S 4BD and
distributed by Penguin Random House UK, 20 Vauxhall Bridge Road,
London SW1V 2SA.

www.randomhouse/everymans
www.everymanslibrary.co.uk

ISBN 978-1-101-90812-9 (US)
978-1-84159-812-3 (UK)

A CIP catalogue reference for this book is available from the
British Library

Library of Congress Cataloging-in-Publication Data

Names: Fragos, Emily, editor.
Title: Poems of Paris / edited by Emily Fragos.
Description: New York: Alfred A. Knopf, [2019] | Series: Everyman's library
pocket poets | "This is a Borzoi book."
Identifiers: LCCN 2018033143 | ISBN 9781101908129 (hardcover: alk. paper)
Subjects: LCSH: Paris (France)—Poetry. | Poetry—Translations into English.
Classification: LCC PN6110.P7 P3563 2019 | DDC 808.81/935844361—dc23
LC record available at https://lccn.loc.gov/2018033143

Typography by Peter B. Willberg

Typeset in the UK by Input Data Services Ltd, Isle Abbotts, Somerset

Printed and bound in Germany by GGP Media GmbH, Pössneck

CONTENTS

THE SIGHTS

THE STREETS

PARISIANS

7

8

12

FOREWORD

Open to any page in this anthology and Paris comes alive, teeming with the denizens of cafés and cabarets, parks and museums, the Left Bank and the Right Bank, narrow side streets and majestic boulevards. People of all sorts parade through these poems: the young and the old, artists and muses, vagabonds and lovers.

To do justice to such a multi-faceted city, I have tried to present a suitably wide variety of poetic voices. Readers will find here not only many representatives of the long and magnificent tradition of French poetry (often rendered into English by translators who are famous poets themselves), but also of the floods of dazzled tourists, long-time visitors, and expatriates who found a home in Paris.

The City of Light has long been an inspiration and a refuge for artists from all over the world: painters, sculptors, jazz geniuses, the Lost Generation of writers, the Beat poets. Impressionism, Symbolism, Cubism, Dadaism, Surrealism – many artistic movements flourished or had their birth in Paris, and that creative ferment is reflected in these pages.

Paris is also the City of Love, "the capital of public kissing," as Billy Collins put it in his poem "January in Paris." It is a place that seems to encourage heightened emotions, which are on full display in a host of poems of tender romance, intense eroticism, and heartbreaking loss. Love of another kind – the Parisians' world-famous delight in fine food and drink – finds room at this table as well.

But aside from love, art, and *joie de vivre*, the specter of war has also haunted Paris's streets. World War II was a time of suffering and survival, of anguish and heroism, portrayed movingly in the poems that conclude this volume. Most notable, perhaps, is Paul Éluard's "Liberté," thousands of copies of which were air-dropped by the British Royal Air Force into occupied France to keep hope alive – a stirring tribute to the real power of poetry.

As hard as it is to contain such an overwhelming and beloved place between two covers, it is my hope that *Poems of Paris* will evoke for its readers, through many moods, eras, and circumstances, the dream that is Paris.

Emily Fragos

THE CITY OF LIGHT

THOUGHT

TRIP TO PARIS

Ah what a charming ride
To leave a gloomy countryside
    For Paris
Lovely Paris
Which long ago
Love must have found beautified
Ah what a charming ride
To leave a gloomy countryside
For Paris

GUILLAUME APOLLINAIRE (1880–1918)   17
TRANSLATED BY ROGER SHATTUCK

From THE PROSE OF THE TRANS-
SIBERIAN AND OF LITTLE JEANNE
OF FRANCE
Dedicated to the musicians

O Paris
Great warm hearth with the intersecting embers of
     your streets and your old houses leaning over
     them for warmth
Like grandmothers
And here are posters in red in green all colors like my
     past in a word yellow
Yellow the proud color of the novels of France
In big cities I like to rub elbows with the buses as they
     go by
Those of the Saint-Germain–Montmartre line that
     carry me to the assault of the Butte
The motors bellow like golden bulls
The cows of dusk graze on Sacré-Coeur
O Paris
Main station where desires arrive at the crossroads of
     restlessness
Now only the paint store has a little light on its door
The International Pullman and Great European
     Express Company has sent me its brochure
It's the most beautiful church in the world
I have friends who surround me like guardrails

They're afraid that when I leave I'll never come back
All the women I've ever known appear around me on
    the horizon
Sometimes the cry of a whistle tears me apart
Over in Manchuria a belly is still heaving, as if giving
    birth
I wish
I wish I'd never started traveling
Tonight a great love is driving me out of my mind
And I can't help thinking about little Jeanne of France.
It's through a sad night that I've written this poem in
    her honor
Jeanne
the little prostitute
I'm sad so sad
I'm going to the Lapin Agile to remember my lost
    youth again
Have a few drinks
And come back home alone

Paris

City of the incomparable Tower the great Gibbet and
    the Wheel

BLAISE CENDRARS (1887–1961)   19
TRANSLATED BY RON PADGETT

TWILIGHT: DAYBREAK

The morning wind rattles the windowpanes
and over the barracks reveille rings out.

Dreams come now, bad dreams, and teen-age boys
burrow into their pillows. Now the lamp
that glowed at midnight seems, like a bloodshot eye,
to throb and throw a red stain on the room;
balked by the stubborn body's weight, the soul
mimics the lamplight's struggles with the dawn.
Like a face in tears – the tears effaced by wind –
the air is tremulous with escaping things,
and Man is tired of writing, Woman of love.

Here and there, chimneys begin to smoke.
Whores, mouths gaping, eyelids gray as ash,
sleep on their feet, leaning against the walls,
and beggar-women, hunched over sagging breasts,
blow on burning sticks, then on their hands.
Now, the hungry feel the cold the worst,
and women in labor suffer the sharpest pains;
now, like a sob cut short by a clot of blood,
a rooster crows somewhere; a sea of mist
swirls around the buildings; in the Hôtel-Dieu
the dying breathe their last, while the debauched,
spent by their exertions, sleep alone.

Shivering dawn, in a wisp of pink and green,
totters slowly across the empty Seine,
and dingy Paris – old drudge rubbing its eyes –
picks up its tools to begin another day.

CHARLES BAUDELAIRE (1821–67)   21
TRANSLATED BY RICHARD HOWARD

THE NOISE OF THE CABARETS ...

The noise of the cabarets, the muck of the sidewalks,
The shrunken plane-trees shedding their leaves in the
    foul air,
The omnibus, hurricane of junk-iron and mud,
That grates, badly seated on its four wheels,
And rolls its eyes slowly red and green,
The workers on their way to the club, puffing
Their stubby pipes at the noses of the police,
Leaky roofs, dripping walls, slippery cobblestones,
Worn-out pavements, gutters overflowing the sewers,
That's how my route lies – with paradise at the end.

PAUL VERLAINE (1844–96)
    TRANSLATED BY KATE FLORES

SPRING EVENING ON THE BOULEVARDS

Sitting on a bench one evening in spring on the great boulevards, near the Variétés. A café streaming with gas. A prostitute dressed all in red going from beer to beer. On the second floor, a room quite somber and quiet with a few lamps and tables over which heads were bent, a little study. On the third floor, adazzle with gas, all the windows open, flowers, perfumes, a dance in progress. One can't hear the music for the din of the street swarming with cabs and people, with the corridors devouring and vomiting people incessantly, and the hawking of programs in front of the Variétés ... But one can see, gliding past in front of these ten windows, men in black tails with white shirt fronts, revolving to the music, holding ladies, blue, pink, lilac, white, holding them ever so lightly, so correctly, one can see them pass, repass, with serious, unsmiling faces (but one can't hear the music they follow). Several pimps wander by; one says to the other: "She made ten francs, old boy ..." From the Variétés a crowd swarms out during intermission; and the hell of the boulevard continues, the cabs, the cafés, the gas, the shopwindows, more and more pedestrians – more prostitutes filing by under the harsh lights of the cafés ... Near me a newspaper stall and two women chatting; one says: "She certainly won't last the night, that one, and my kid caught it from hers." Busses filled with members of both sexes, each with his or her own feelings, troubles, vices.

And above it all, the gentle, eternal stars.

TRANSLATED BY WILLIAM JAY SMITH

PARIS IN SPRING

The city's all a-shining
Beneath a fickle sun,
A gay young wind's a-blowing,
The little shower is done.
But the rain-drops still are clinging
And falling one by one –
Oh it's Paris, it's Paris,
And spring-time has begun.

I know the Bois is twinkling
In a sort of hazy sheen,
And down the Champs the gray old arch
Stands cold and still between.
But the walk is flecked with sunlight
Where the great acacias lean,
Oh it's Paris, it's Paris,
And the leaves are growing green.

The sun's gone in, the sparkle's dead,
There falls a dash of rain,
But who would care when such an air
Comes blowing up the Seine?
And still Ninette sits sewing
Beside her window-pane,
When it's Paris, it's Paris,
And spring-time's come again.

SARA TEASDALE (1884–1933)

"PARIS; THIS APRIL SUNSET COMPLETELY UTTERS"

Paris;this April sunset completely utters
utters serenely silently a cathedral

before whose upward lean magnificent face
the streets turn young with rain,

spiral acres of bloated rose
coiled within cobalt miles of sky
yield to and heed
the mauve
              of twilight(who slenderly descends,
daintily carrying in her eyes the dangerous first stars)
people move love hurry in a gently

arriving gloom and
see!(the new moon
fills abruptly with sudden silver
these torn pockets of lame and begging colour)while
there and here the lithe indolent prostitute
Night,argues

with certain houses

PARIS AT NIGHT

It's not a city, it's a world

– It is the sea: dead calm – and the spring tide
With a far-off roaring has departed.
The surge will come back rolling in its noise –
Do you hear the scratching of the crabs of night?

– It is the Styx run dry: The ragpicker Diogenes,
Lantern in hand, roams about unperturbed.
All along the black stream depraved poets
Fish; from empty skulls they bait their lines.

– It is the field: To glean the dirty rags
The turning flight of hideous Harpies swoops;
The alley cat, on the lookout for rats,
Flees Bondy's criminal sons, nocturnal vintagers.

– It is death: Here lie the police. – Up there, love
Siestas, sucking the meat of a heavy arm
Where the quenched kiss leaves its red mark . . .
The hour is alone – Listen . . . not a dream is moving.

– It is life: Listen: the live stream is singing
The eternal song on the slimy head
Of a sea-god stretching his limbs naked and green
On a bed of the Morgue . . . With his eyes wide open!

TRISTAN CORBIÈRE (1845–75)   27
TRANSLATED BY KENNETH KOCH
AND GEORGES GUY

SQUARE D'ORLÉANS

A place where pain and beauty
mingled once – two substances
that have long been acquainted.
A bank now occupies this space;
dapper gentlemen enter and exit,
each one slim as a new banknote.

Chopin lived here once. His fingers
struck the keyboard, matter, in a rage.
Impassioned poetry once lived here.
Peace and quiet now prevail, while nearby
insurance agents flourish, and the doctor
receives his patients at appointed hours.

Dusk falls; apartment houses stand
like worried herons on the century's rubble
(the distant whistle of the city sounds).
In the center of the square a little fountain
shyly raises up two braids of water,
reminding us of what life really is.

We sit on the steps as nothing happens.
It's also impossible to say
that we feel anything like sorrow.
Anxiety and frenzy (two
younger nations) have given way
to classical restraint.

The September evening slowly darkens,
a gentle wind traverses Paris
like an elderly Kabuki actor
playing the ingenue's part.
If anything upsets us – but nothing
does – it's only emptiness.

ADAM ZAGAJEWSKI (1945–)

29

TRANSLATED BY CLARE CAVANAGH

PARIS

It's true, I love Paris with mawkish tenderness.
Go where I may, I miss the old banks of the Seine.
When I'm beside the sea, or viewing snowy peaks,
I dream of neighborhoods where swarms of children
    play,
Of a bald knoll from which my Muse appreciates
The subtle variegations of a somber sky,
Of Bièvre's shoreline, with some half-forgotten tracts
Where people stretch a cord between scrub-poplar
    trunks
For hanging flannel clothes and bedding out to dry,
Or of a fishing-hole on the isle of Grenelle.

30   FRANÇOIS COPPÉE (1842–1908)
TRANSLATED BY KENDALL LAPPIN

HORIZON
to Tristan Tzara

The whole town has come into my room
the trees have disappeared
and evening clings to my fingers
The houses are turning into ocean liners
the sound of the sea has just reached me up here
In two days we'll arrive in the Congo
I've passed the Equator and the Tropic of Capricorn
I know there are innumerable hills
Notre-Dame hides the Gaurisankar and the Northern
    Lights
night falls drop by drop
I wait for the hours

Give me that lemonade and a last cigarette
I'm going back to Paris

PHILIPPE SOUPAULT (1897–1990)   31
TRANSLATED BY ROSMARIE WALDROP

PARIS

never
even in calmer times
have I ever
dreamed of
bicycling through that
city
wearing a
beret

and
Camus
always
pissed
me
off.

PARIS IS MY SEROQUEL

Long may I savor your organ meats
and stinky cheeses, endure your pompous
manners, breathe your gentle gardens,
wake up – beyond boredom and daydream –
to your vast gray skies, I, smiling politely
at so many dull faces passing by,
I, who am normally so restrictive,
except in relation to him I once loved
(now worn and dangerous), each day,
kneeling down, I, as some strange energy
penetrates my forehead, I, striving to draw
nearer to you, and to your stones, I, without
    nervousness
or regret, as all the gold of the world seems to stroke
my haunches and hooves.

CLEANLINESS

The little pigeons full of whimsicrap
used to come and go flying over Paris
giving its walls an exquisite shade
of avian poop grayish in tint
never suspecting poor innocents
that a devious plot waits for them below

now they are trapped!
they are not happy

adieu Paris! adieu my beautiful city
says the pigeon sent off to the country
I will no longer crap on your Hôtel de Ville
I will no longer crap on your proud monuments
such sadness, I weep to think of it,
to waste such fine excrement
which could have buttered the homes
of my native city eating away at the cement
brick concrete marble flint
yes, cries the pigeon to himself, I am quite proud
my turds are virulent PH acid
adieu my beautiful Paris adieu my dear city
I leave for my exile in a paddy wagon
I will forever retain amidst the hicks
the indelible image of the charm of your streets

34   RAYMOND QUENEAU (1903–76)
    TRANSLATED BY RACHEL GALVIN

PARIS

Childcity, Aprilcity,
Spirits of angels crouched in doorways,
Poets, worms in hair, beautiful Baudelaire,
Artaud, Rimbaud, Apollinaire,
Look to the nightcity –
Informers and concierges,
Montparnassian woe, deathical Notre Dame,
To the nightcircle look, dome heirloomed,
Hugo and Zola together entombed,
Harlequin deathtrap,
Seine generates ominous mud,
Eiffel looks down – sees the Apocalyptical ant crawl,
New Yorkless city,
City of Germans dead and gone,
Dollhouse of Mama War.

HAS PARIS CHANGED?

The full moon in her silk panties comes out
Over la Place Vendôme. Edith Piaf sings
Down in a basement bar on la Rue Jacob

Where I have a room with a sink, hot water
After nineteen hours. Like all my fellow
Students – Spaniards, South Africans, French, Poles

(Escaped from Warsaw) – I zigzag to the Sorbonne
Where I study *philo* and *philosophie*.
We are all poor and rich, studying full time,

Eating at l'École des Mines down three flights,
Worst, cheapest food in our *arrondissement*.
With French, Dutch, Hungarian, Yankee poets

We launch *Points*, a literary mag and I read often at
Les Deux Magots. Motorcycles roar outside
To drown us out. We chase after them, hitting

Them with chunks of ice, beer cans. Some of us wed.
Some with many war memories break down.
Are buildings the same? Along la Rue Bonaparte,

Stone walls, intimate windows with books and
    big-eyed
Japanese wood dolls. Rare letters signed by Voltaire,
Napoléon, Guillaume Apollinaire and James Joyce

Appear like rare medieval fish engraved brown
In bestiaries, all in the fine handwriting of
Our 18th century *Declaration of Independence.*

A desperate phone call and I buy a coarse jacket
At Au Bon Marché, 10 dollars, a week's rent,
To give to Singh, a pal from Mumbai, who needs

It quick for a forced wedding at the Mairie.
In tenebrous winter Paris, I walk in icy rain.
Paris never changes. Look around. Take a bus.

The full moon in her silk panties comes out
Over la Place Vendôme. Edith Piaf sings
Down in a basement bar on la Rue Jacob.

PARIS IS BEYOND COMPARE

When I've gone round the earth and sea
and visited all places, every one,
seen Egypt and Jerusalem and Galilee,
Damascus, Alexandria and Babylon,
Cairo and Syria and Tartary,
and entered every port,
and seen the spices and the sweets that they make
    there,
although they're better than the French have got,
Paris is beyond compare.

She is the city crowned above the rest,
the fount of scholarship and wisdom, and its well,
located on the river Seine, possessed
of woods and vineyards, land and dell.
She has more of the mortal good that we embrace
than any other place;
all strangers love her, will always find her fair,
because such elegance, such happiness,
will not be found in any town but this:
Paris is beyond compare.

For she's much better than any fortress town:
she has chateaux built in the days of old,
she's peopled with merchants, men of renown,
and workers of every kind, in armour, gold;
the flower of all the arts, as you've heard tell;
her workmen all excel;
deep understanding and a subtle skill
was found in her inhabitants, and is found still,
and loyalty to the craft that's in their care:
Paris is beyond compare.

EUSTACHE DESCHAMPS (1346–1406)   39
TRANSLATED BY DAVID CURZON AND
JEFFREY FISKIN

THE SIGHTS

THE STORY

MONTMARTRE

Pigalle:
A neon rose
In a champagne bottle.
At dawn
The petals
Fall.

LE JARDIN DES TUILERIES

This winter air is keen and cold,
   And keen and cold this winter sun,
   But round my chair the children run
Like little things of dancing gold.

Sometimes about the painted kiosk
   The mimic soldiers strut and stride,
   Sometimes the blue-eyed brigands hide
In the bleak tangles of the bosk.

And sometimes, while the old nurse cons
   Her book, they steal across the square,
   And launch their paper navies where
Huge Triton writhes in greenish bronze.

And now in mimic flight they flee,
   And now they rush, a boisterous band –
   And, tiny hand on tiny hand,
Climb up the black and leafless tree.

Ah! cruel tree! if I were you,
   And children climbed me, for their sake
   Though it be winter I would break
Into spring blossoms white and blue!

OSCAR WILDE (1854–1900)

TO THE EIFFEL TOWER

All right now, Eiffel Tower, stop giving me the eye
    like that.
If I present you with a sonnet in correct fourteeners
(A meter Jacques Réda has toiled assiduously at)
It doesn't give the right to meter me with your
    crabbed eye

Meters you have, it's true, and also have the color drab
(I think the French would call it "terne") in common
    with the crab
In spite of the Mercurochrome (lead oxide, red) with
    which
The city disinfects your scratches from the wind and
    sand.

A dense crowd amble in the area your four legs straddle
And gawk up at your nether parts. Should you not
    hide your ass?
(Ass theoretical, it's true) but children are not banned

And will go back directly to our countryside and
    dream
Perverted ever after – love, but for a giantess
Like quite unquiet hamlets lying at the mountain's
    foot.

JACQUES ROUBAUD (1932–)   45
TRANSLATED BY KEITH AND ROSMARIE WALDROP

LES INVALIDES

At dusk by Les Invalides
a few old men play at boules,
holding the crouch
long after the toss, listening for the clack
of steel on steel, strolling over and studying the
     ground.

At boules, it is the creaking grace, the slow amble,
     the stillness,
the dusk deepening,
a plane tree casting loose a few leaves,
shadows lying behind the undistracted eyes.

It is empty cots lined up
in the darkness of rooms where the last true men
listen each dusk
for the high, thin clack
sounding from the home village very far away.

PLACE DU CARROUSEL

Place du Carrousel
toward the end of a beautiful summer's day
the blood of a horse
hit and unhitched
streamed
on the pavement
And the horse was there
standing
still
on three feet
And the other foot hurt
hurt and torn
hung down
Close to him
standing
still
was also the cabby
and then the cab
it also still
useless as a broken clock
And the horse was silent
the horse was not complaining
the horse was not neighing
he was there
he was waiting

and he was so handsome so sad so simple
and so reasonable
it was impossible to hold back the tears
Oh
lost gardens
forgotten fountains
prairies in sun
oh suffering
splendor and mystery of adversity
blood and flickered light
stricken beauty
Fraternity.

TRANSLATED BY LAWRENCE FERLINGHETTI

ARC DE TRIOMPHE

Two lover trees
two pecans in a field

or maybe twins who sustained
the same height & chiral joined at the top

parading wind
sheltering cattle

FADY JOUDAH (1971–)

IN A STATION OF THE MÉTRO

The apparition of these faces in the crowd;
Petals on a wet, black bough.

NOTRE DAME

Where a Roman judged a foreign people
A basilica stands and, first and joyful
Like Adam once, an arch plays with its own ribs:
Groined, muscular, never unnerved.

From outside, the bones betray the plan:
Here flying buttresses ensure
That cumbersome mass shan't crush the walls –
A vault bold as a battering-ram is idle.

Elemental labyrinth, unfathomable forest,
The Gothic soul's rational abyss,
Egyptian power and Christian shyness,
Oak together with reed – and perpendicular as tsar.

But the more attentively I studied,
Notre Dame, your monstrous ribs, your stronghold,
The more I thought: I too one day shall create
Beauty from cruel weight.

1912

TRANSLATED BY JAMES GREENE

BASTILLE DAY

The first time I saw Paris
I went to see where the Bastille
had been, and though
I saw the column there
I was too aware that
the Bastille was not there:
I did not know how
to see the emptiness.
People go to see
the missing Twin Towers
and seem to like feeling
the lack of something.
I do not like knowing
that my mother no longer
exists, or the feeling
of knowing. Excuse me
for comparing my mother
to large buildings. Also
for talking about absence.
The red and gray sky
above the rooftops
is darkening and the inhabitants
are hastening home for dinner.
I hope to see you later.

RON PADGETT (1942–)

SLEEPING ON THE CEILING

It is so peaceful on the ceiling!
It is the Place de la Concorde.
The little crystal chandelier
is off, the fountain is in the dark.
Not a soul is in the park.

Below, where the wallpaper is peeling,
the Jardin des Plantes has locked its gates.
Those photographs are animals.
The mighty flowers and foliage rustle;
under the leaves the insects tunnel.

We must go under the wallpaper
to meet the insect-gladiator,
to battle with a net and trident,
and leave the fountain and the square.
But oh, that we could sleep up there ...

THE SEINE IN PARIS

Since I prefer rivers to regrets
the grave profundity of monuments to memories,
love the water's flow dividing cities,
the Seine in Paris knows me deeply faithful
to its gentle book-lined quays. Not a breath
arrives defeated by the eddying waters
but that I am ready to take it and to read again
in its hair the mountain song, not a
summer night-time silence but that I glide
like a leaf between air and water, not a white
gull's wing returned from the sea pursuing the sun
but that I am wrenched from the weight of my
    monotony
by a strident cry! The pillars weigh heavy
after the unnecessary step and I plunge
by them to earth, and when I climb up again
streaming and shake myself,
I invoke a god who looks through windows
and gleams with pleasure in the panes.
Protected by his rays I conduct an inner race
with water which will not wait
and from the burden of footsteps and motorcar noises
the beating of hammers on bars and voices
that rapid flow frees me ... Quaysides
and towers are already far away when

suddenly I rediscover them, covering like the
    centuries,
with equal love and equal terror, wave upon wave,
meanderings of the mind and the bend of my river.

54   JEAN TARDIEU (1903—95)
    TRANSLATED BY DAVID KELLEY

AT THE ÉTOILE
(*At the Unknown Soldier's Grave in Paris*)

If in the lists of life he bore him well,
Sat gracefully or fell unhorsed in love,
No tongue is dowered now with speech to tell
Since he and death somewhere matched glove with
     glove.

What proud or humble union gave him birth,
Not reckoning on this immortal bed,
Is one more riddle that the cryptic earth
Though knowing chooses to retain unsaid.

Since he was weak as other men, – or like
Young Galahad as fair in thought as limb,
Each bit of moving dust in France may strike
Its breast in pride, knowing he stands for him.

COUNTEE CULLEN (1903–46)

THE STREETS

From ARRONDISSEMENTS

In Paris there are twenty arrondissements
There are also "three-or-four hundred lassies"
According to the song
If "three hundred" it's fifteen per arrondissement
If "four hundred" they average twenty
In any case not many
And I have never seen them "dance among the
      grassies."

The twenty arrondissements of Paris are numbered
Nr. 1 is called the Ist Arrondissement
Nr. 2 is called the IInd,
And so on (up to twenty).

In the Ist arrondissement is the main post office in
Rue du Louvre. You can mail your letters there; even
on Sunday. That is very convenient.

The IInd arrondissement is remarkable because it
houses (and will at least till 1998) the Bibliothèque
Nationale.

In the IIIrd arrondissement you will find "the verd-
ant Square des Arts et des Métiers." A character in the
novel *Les copains* by Mr. Farigoule (alias Jules Romain)
announces that he is about to go there "on the gadget
that accelerates the feet."

The IVth arrondissement is known for the BHV department store.

The Vth for its Panthéon, "a jewel of Gothic art."

Of the VIth we'll remember the Luxembourg Gardens and its statues. Raymond Queneau has drawn up a quasi exhaustive list of them in *Courir les rues* (a book of poems by that author).

The VIIth is towered over by the Eiffel Tower.

The VIIIth by the Arc de Triomphe.

In the IXth is the present residence of M. Roubaud who is composing the present prose poem.

The Xth arrondissement is cut through by the canal Saint-Martin where once was the Hotel du Nord whose famous "atmosphere" we know. Is it also here that Louis Jouvet made, to my mind no less famously, this definitive statement: *"Les mères de famille vous disent 'mère . . . de famille.'"*

The XIth arrondissement is not the location of the CHU Saint-Antoine Hospital where Georges Perec worked.

This CHU is in the XIIth (unless I'm mistaken; in which case it's *vice versa* or *Lycée de Versailles* as Pierre Dac used to say (unless it was Francis Blanche)).

In the XIIIth I'll point out the Park Montsouris and its Eastern boundary, the Rue Gazan where François Caradec of the Oulipo lives.

The XIVth has the street of la Tombe-Issoire, but

not the street of la Folie-Méricourt (which is in the XIth).

The XVth is far, very far. In its Rue des Favorites is the Center for Postal Money Orders.

The XVIth arrondissement has Pomp. Rue de la.

Entering the XVIIth one thinks of Aristide Bruant and his song (I quote from memory, poorly) *"La morale de cette histoir'là / d'cette histoir'là / c'est que les filles qu'a pas d'papa / qu'a pas d'papa 'faut pas les envoyer à l'école / aux Batignolles."*

The XVIIIth is the Butte.

The XIXth is feeling for nature (at the Buttes-Chaumont, obviously).

And now we finally get to the XXth arrondissement. We go to the Mur des Fédérés (not many visitors).

RUE DES ÉCOUFFES
For Marie-Geneviève Havel

The street is narrow, and it just extends
rue de Rivoli / rue des Rosiers
a street from which the children went away
clutching their mothers, looking for their friends –
on city buses used for other ends
one not-yet-humid morning in July.
Now kosher butchers co-exist with gay
boutiques, not gaily. Smooth-cheeked ephebes hold
    hands.
Small boys with forelocks trail after bearded men –
and I have dragged that story in again
and will inevitably next compare
the curtains of the creaky balcony
smelling of female exile, exhaled prayer
with the discreet shutters of the women's bar.

BYPASSING RUE DESCARTES

Bypassing rue Descartes
I descended toward the Seine, shy, a traveler,
A young barbarian just come to the capital of the
    world.

We were many, from Jassy and Koloshvar, Wilno and
    Bucharest, Saigon and Marrakesh,
Ashamed to remember the customs of our homes,
About which nobody here should ever be told:
The clapping for servants, barefooted girls hurry in,
Dividing food with incantations,
Choral prayers recited by master and household
    together.

I had left the cloudy provinces behind,
I entered the universal, dazzled and desiring.

Soon enough, many from Jassy and Koloshvar, or
    Saigon or Marrakesh
Would be killed because they wanted to abolish the
    customs of their homes.

Soon enough, their peers were seizing power
In order to kill in the name of the universal, beautiful
    ideas.

Meanwhile the city behaved in accordance with its
    nature,
Rustling with throaty laughter in the dark,
Baking long breads and pouring wine into clay
    pitchers,
Buying fish, lemons, and garlic at street markets,
Indifferent as it was to honor and shame and greatness
    and glory,
Because that had been done already and had
    transformed itself
Into monuments representing nobody knows whom,
Into arias hardly audible and into turns of speech.

Again I lean on the rough granite of the embankment,
As if I had returned from travels through the
    underworlds
And suddenly saw in the light the reeling wheel of the
    seasons
Where empires have fallen and those once living are
    now dead.

There is no capital of the world, neither here nor
    anywhere else,
And the abolished customs are restored to their small
    fame
And now I know that the time of human generations is
    not like the time of the earth.

As to my heavy sins, I remember one most vividly:
How, one day, walking on a forest path along a stream,
I pushed a rock down onto a water snake coiled in the
    grass.

And what I have met with in life was the just
    punishment
Which reaches, sooner or later, the breaker of a taboo.

Berkeley, 1980

BEAT HOTEL, 9 RUE GÎT-LE-COEUR

... appalling, it reeked
of butts (Gauloises and
human) ... stale wine ... bohemians
leaning against pocked walls
marked with their scent ... in grey
rooms ... Gendarmes eye them,
at the entrance to the
bistro, suspiciously. Smoke-
stained white chenille curtains
drawn to keep out snoops.
Something strange about this place,
they'd mutter, scowling
at tourists and surrealists:
évidemment sales étrangers ...
disreputable foreigners, hein.
Days of rage in Paris ... *toujours*
with a kalashnikoff look,
a Molotov cocktail temper,
or an Uzi up your nose.
We're looking for someone, *monsieur,*
who could be you. *Dîtes-donc, alors.*
You don't say. Just keep
your mouth shut, speak
no French, and fade away.

From STREETS

A house with the façade painted yellow, in the sunshine, a dejected-looking woman with her head bowed at a window.

A policeman and some navvies are standing around in the street. The red wine from the vineyards of Le Hérault and Algeria flows in the wine-shops, where serving girls, perspiring a little, laugh, sponge oilcloths and polish the splendid zinc at the bar.

The solitary tree in the Parisian courtyard is bedecked with Île-de-France green, blending with the most sumptuous grey.

Conversations come at us from all sides. Vulgarities give you such a strong feeling of life that you feel like hugging the women who utter them, on the street and in their homes as well, beside their little polished stoves. In the air human smells mix with those smells of vinegar, onions, frying; they issue from open windows, windows which look out on to the Sacré-Cœur, Notre-Dame or a graveyard.

Every day you can transcribe on to the harsh slate of everyday life a marvellous *Carte de Tendre.* You would have to include on it the painted rose above the door of a brothel in Grenelle in the midday sun, the obscure graffiti on the wall of a local church built in the Second Empire, the gesture of a street urchin who, as though to pluck a delicious moment from the air, with fingers splayed, spreads out the palm of his grubby little hand on the burning hot wall.

Desolate walkers peer at saucy postcards, the soles of their shoes are wearing out. Cold or hot rain made large holes in them as big as royal *écus*.

In the newly-green squares mothers open their corsages to nurse their babies, a small piece of silver braid shines on the collar of the park keeper's tunic. In the grocers' shops the assistants fill grey sacks with rock salt. In the doorway of her dairy a woman sucks the blood from a small cut on her finger. Locksmiths are cutting and filing keys. The tripe sellers display their calves' hearts on the marble slabs.

Wide-eyed matrons and young housewives who feel the cold, their satiny skin getting worn away gradually beneath woollen garments, buy products of the chemical industry from the hardware shop: bleach, cats' head soap and soap veined red and blue ... On café terraces a dash of syrup makes a fleetingly delicate cloud in the sparkling aperitif, a glass smashes, a child cries.

Silence fills a whole street, on which, through a window, you can see a girl with a naked back washing herself.

It happens that you sometimes walk along streets without any charm or distinction, which remain, as it were, abstracted, where night comes down more simply, where the hours chime more clearly, streets which are suddenly made famous by a mysterious murder.

In some of them, with turn-of-the-century façades, adorned with identical balconies, in rooms decorated in garish colours melancholic couples give themselves up to the pleasures of the flesh amid the faded furniture: the evening newspaper is opened on a chair, the mice gnaw at a piece of Gruyère abandoned in a saucer. All these things are part and parcel of a night in Paris, the wind blowing as it used to blow in the old days, when the *chouans* went out reconnoitring under a starless sky.

JEAN FOLLAIN (1903–71)

TRANSLATED BY HELEN CONSTANTINE

LA RUE RAVIGNAN

"You can't bathe in the same river twice," said the philosopher Heraclitus. But here it's always the same ones climbing the street. Happy or sad, they go by at the same times. I've named all of you who walk the rue Ravignan for famous dead people. Here's Agamemnon. There's Mme. Hanska! Ulysses is the milkman! Patroclus lives down the street! Castor and Pollux are the ladies on the fifth floor. But you, old ragman, who come to take the still-unspoiled scraps in the magic morning when I'm turning off my big good lamp, you that I don't know, mysterious poor ragpicker, I've given you a celebrated name: I call you Dostoevsky!

70   MAX JACOB (1876–1944)
     TRANSLATED BY WILLIAM T. KULIK

AT SAINT-GERMAIN

At Saint-Germain-des-Prés, with its three cafés, its
serious stores, spacious and indifferent to the street
and where you don't wait in line to go in, with its
stuffed newspaper stand, its sad-looking banks, its
square always in the shade, its goldsmiths and large
photographic gallery, which seem to recruit their cli-
entele in Roumergue, Saumur, Vitré, Switzerland; at
Saint-Germain-des-Prés, where are opposed and
joined intellectual refinement and the purest melan-
choly of the not yet evolved bourgeois, I am most
of the time intoxicated with the simple sensation of
existing; with the honest certainty of playing a role,
not providential but solid and real, turning in a circle,
in the true life of Paris. I have friends there who are
not the same at Lipp's, at Flore, at the Deux Magots,
who aren't merely the paleographer, the novelist, the
actor or the broker, but artisans, simple beings,
passers-by, the fellow who sells lottery tickets, the
plumber....

Do you want me to say that there I saw Picasso,
Gaston Leroux, Carco, Giraudoux, naval officers, the
Guimet museum, all kinds of academies, Aragon,
Saint-Exupéry, Gertrude Stein, petroleum, business,
sports, Rainer Maria Rilke ... there's no end. Espe-
cially I see there my life, my hasty dinners at Lipp's

71

where today they're expecting the return of Münster cheese and Saveloy with the sharp sauce; I see my articles consigned to paper at the moment they begin to sweep under the feet of the habitués, the times on the way home from Pleyel or Gaveau, those brief stops, sad but rewarding you make in front of a drink. In my memories I have smells of overcoats, dogs passing under the tables, noises of saucers mingled with government collapses, the wrath of clocks, laughter of pretty women fallen there like feathers of turtle doves, rounds of theories which were to fix or upset everything, handshakes confused with a distraught and peaceful state of mind, inflated, whispering, warm and almost salutary, which is like the mind of the highest steeple.

Beloved Saint-Germain-des-Prés, where adventurous failures and artistic scatterbrains have the exceptional chance of sipping their glass of brandy between a prince of the intellect and a movie villain, under the knowing and vaguely desperate eyes of those modern young girls to whom Richepin, in his proud youth of poet-vagabond, used to say from behind his beard: "It's too early for adultery!" Rue de l'Abbaye, rue du Dragon, Hôtel Taranne, rue Saint-Benoît, art book stores, concierges, seamsters, dry-salters, art dealers on the rue Bonaparte, second-hand dealers, upholsterers, repairers of candelabra, umbrellas, porcelain, the Corsican restaurant, pharmacies, a center of talk where you found the time, at the most Teutonic curfew, to rage against bourgeois thinking in front of a poisonous glass of beer ... delightful parade speaking to my heart. That is where I drank a last glass with so many departed friends whose memory weighs on my soul with all the bitter faithful softness of the dead.

LÉON-PAUL FARGUE (1876–1947)   73
TRANSLATED BY WALLACE FOWLIE

PARISIANS

BALLADE OF FORGIVENESS

Brothers and sisters, Celestine,
Carthusian, or Carmelite,
Street-loafers, fops whose buckles shine,
Lackeys, and courtesans whose tight
Apparel gratifies the sight,
And little ladies'-men who trot
In tawny boots of dreadful height:
I beg forgiveness of the lot.

Young whores who flash their teats in sign
Of what they hawk for men's delight,
Ape-handlers, thieves and, soused with wine,
Wild bullies looking for a fight,
And Jacks and Jills whose hearts are light,
Whistling and joking, talking rot,
Street-urchins dodging left and right:
I beg forgiveness of the lot.

Excepting for those bloody swine
Who gave me, many a morn and night,
The hardest crusts on which to dine;
Henceforth I'll fear them not a mite.

I'd belch and fart in their despite,
Were I not sitting on my cot.
Well, to be peaceful and polite,
I beg forgiveness of the lot.

May hammers, huge and heavy, smite
Their ribs, and likewise cannon-shot.
May cudgels pulverize them quite.
I beg forgiveness of the lot.

STREET CIRCUS

In the middle of that crowd there is a child who is dancing, a man lifting weights. His arms with blue tattoos call on the sky to witness their useless strength.

The child dances, lightly, in tights too big for him, lighter than the balls he's balancing himself on. And when he passes the hat, no one gives anything. No one gives for fear of making it too heavy. He is so thin.

PIERRE REVERDY (1889–1960)   79
TRANSLATED BY RON PADGETT

THE MIME

By what extraordinary, crazy whim did I
Come to grimace one night before my mirror's eye,
One chill late-autumn night when Paris, dark and
    bleak,
Was glumly sucking up the mists from off the Seine?

The fact is that by mixing tenderness with hate,
Astonishment with rage, and laughter with despair,
My physiognomy, reflected in the glass,
Played every single key of human mimicry;

And as I concentrated with sincerity
On rendering with keenest, strictest verity
The rictus of a demon cursing his black art,

I saw framed in the mirror's glaucous, naked light,
Instead of my own face, a visage strange to me,
Wherein there flashed my own true personality!

CLOCHARD

In Paris, on a day that stayed morning until dusk,
in a Paris like –
in a Paris which –
(save me, sacred folly of description!) Clochard
in a garden by a stone cathedral
(bit built, no, rather
played upon a lute)
a clochard, a lay monk, a naysayer
sleeps sprawled like a knight in effigy.

If he ever owned anything, he has lost it,
and having lost it doesn't want it back.
He's still owed soldier's pay for the conquest of
    Gaul –
but he's got over that, it doesn't matter.
And they never paid him in the fifteenth century
for posing as the thief on Christ's left hand –
he has forgotten all about it, he's not waiting.

He earns his red wine
by trimming the neighborhood dogs.
He sleeps with the air of an inventor of dreams,
his thick beard swarming towards the sun.

The gray chimeras (to wit, bulldogryphons,
hellephants, hippopotoads, croakodilloes,
        rhinocerberuses,
behemammoths, and demonopods,
that omnibestial Gothic allegro vivace)
unpetrify

and examine him with a curiosity
they never turn on me or you,
prudent Peter,
zealous Michael,
enterprising Eve,
Barbara, Clare.

THE ISLAND WOMEN OF PARIS

skim from curb to curb like regatta,
from Pont Neuf to the Quai de la Rappe
in cool negotiation with traffic,
each a country to herself
transposed to this city
by a fluke called "imperial courtesy."

The island women glide past held aloft
by a wire running straight to heaven.
Who can ignore their ornamental bearing,
turbans haughty as parrots,
or deft braids carved into airy cages
transfixed on their manifest brows?

The island women move through Paris
as if they had just finished inventing
their destinations. It's better
not to get in their way. And better
not look an island woman in the eye –
unless you like feeling unnecessary.

RITA DOVE (1952–)

THE GRIFFIN

I am a memory that fails to reach the threshold
I wander in limbos where the gleam of absinthe
when the heart of night breathes through its vents
flicks the fallen star wherein we see ourselves

The sky of our creole has taken on its creamy new
      consistency
of freshly
opened coconut

O spitting Andes and sacred Mayumbe
sole wreck suborned by our eye's fine ship
when with soul mad lacerated mad
   through clouds that come close-serried in the fish
I reascend to haunt the sinister thickness of things

84   AIMÉ CÉSAIRE (1913–2008)
TRANSLATED BY GREGSON DAVIS

THE BUS DRIVER

What has gotten into the bus driver
Who has left his bus, who has sat down
On a curb on the Place de l'Opéra
Where he slips into the ease of being
Nothing more than his own tears? The passers-by
Who bend over such a shared and
Presentable sorrow would like him
To tell them that the wind used to know
How to come out of the woods towards a woman's
    dress,
Or that one day his brother said to him
Even your shadow wants nothing to do with you.
His feet in a puddle, the bus driver
Can only repeat: *This work is hard
And people aren't kind.*

HÉDI KADDOUR (1945–)   85
TRANSLATED BY MARILYN HACKER

THE GREAT LAMENT OF MY OBSCURITY THREE

where we live the flowers of the clocks catch fire and the
plumes encircle the brightness
in the distant sulphur morning the cows lick the salt
    lilies
my son
my son
let us always scuff along through the colour of the
    world
that looks bluer than the métro and astronomy
we are too skinny
we have no mouth
our legs are stiff and knock together
our faces have no form like the stars
crystal points without strength fire the mad basilica
burned: the zigzags crack
telephone
bite the rigging liquefy
the arc
climb
astral
memory
towards the north through its double fruit
like raw flesh
hunger fire blood

RAIN ALL NIGHT, PARIS

On the road home the tide is rising.

Riding the road-tide is dangerous
but it's not safe to stand still.
Hang on the verge & you drown.

I'm going along for the ride.
I may see more riders further on.
Drowning must wait till I get there

and who knows who might be waiting
with a flashlight, a thermos,
even a raft or canoe.

BLIND

Beyond the last window
The bells of the Sacré-Coeur
Make the leaves fall

     ON THE SUMMIT

        A BLIND MAN

Eyelids full of music
Raises his hands
      in the midst of the void

She who comes from afar
Has not given him her arm

He is all alone

      And with his broken voice

He sings a melody
      that no one
          has understood

88   VICENTE HUIDOBRO (1893–1948)
TRANSLATED BY L. C. BREUNIG

A PATH IN THE LUXEMBOURG

She passed me by, that young lady
Lithe and lively as a bird:
In her hand a shimmering bloom,
On her lips the freshest tune.

Might it be she of all in the world
Whose heart alone might answer mine,
Who'd venture into my dark night
And with one look, fill it with light!

But no, my youth has been and gone ...
Farewell sweet beam that on me shone, –
Scent, young lady, harmony ...
Joy passed me by, – escaping me!

GÉRARD DE NERVAL (1808–55)   89
TRANSLATED BY OLIVIA McCANNON

DREAM OF FEBRUARY 11, 19—

I'm in a café; a café in Paris, like the one near the
Métro Liège where I go every morning to read the
paper and have breakfast. It is morning (a young blond
woman is moving a wet mop between the tables, under
the customers' feet, under mine) but it is still dark. I
spread the paper in front of me; the owner comes and
puts an "au lait" on the table and two slices of bread
and butter; he takes the two ten franc coins that I fish
out of my pocket and gives me one franc eighty
change. Somebody comes in.

DREAM OF AUGUST 17, 19—

I'm in a café; a café in Paris, like the one near the
Métro Liège where I go every morning to read the
paper and have breakfast. It is morning (a young blond
woman is moving a wet mop between the tables, under
the customers' feet, under mine) but it is not dark. I
spread the paper in front of me; the owner comes and
puts an "au lait" on the table and two slices of bread
and butter; he takes the two ten franc coins that I fish
out of my pocket and gives me one franc twenty
change. Somebody comes in.

90   JACQUES ROUBAUD (1932–)
     TRANSLATED BY KEITH AND
     ROSMARIE WALDROP

THE CITY OF LOVE

I HAVE DREAMED OF YOU SO MUCH

I have dreamed of you so much that you are no longer real.

Is there still time for me to reach your breathing body, to kiss your mouth and make your dear voice come alive again?

I have dreamed of you so much that my arms, grown used to being crossed on my chest as I hugged your shadow, would perhaps not bend to the shape of your body.

For faced with the real form of what has haunted me and governed me for so many days and years, I would surely become a shadow.

O scales of feeling.

I have dreamed of you so much that surely there is no more time for me to wake up. I sleep on my feet, prey to all the forms of life and love, and you, the only one who counts for me today, I can no more touch your face and lips than touch the lips and face of some passerby.

I have dreamed of you so much, have walked so much, talked so much, slept so much with your phantom, that perhaps the only thing left for me is to become a phantom among phantoms, a shadow a hundred times more shadow than the shadow that moves and goes on moving, brightly, over the sundial of your life.

ROBERT DESNOS (1900–45)   93
TRANSLATED BY PAUL AUSTER

From *SONNETS POUR HÉLÈNE* (40)

As you understand clearly that I hungrily feed
On the glance of your eyes, whose rays I steal,
A thief, to feed the sadness which rules over me,
Why do you hide from me those eyes by which you
    please me?

You have twice come to Paris, yet you pretend
Never to come here, so that my suffering
Is not lessened in seeing your eyes as I desire,
Your eyes which feed me through the sting of their
    rays.

You even go to Hercueil with your cousin
To see the meadows, gardens and the spring next
To the cave where I sang so many varying songs.

You should have called for me, forgetful mistress;
Carried in your coach I'd not have made much of a
    crowd
For I am no longer anything but a ghost without a
    body.

94   PIERRE DE RONSARD (1524–85)
    TRANSLATED BY PROSPER BLANCHEMAIN

From ZONE

Now you walk in Paris all alone in the crowd
Beside you lowing buses sway like cattle in a herd
Love-sickness makes a lump in your throat
As if you were never again to be loved
Once you would have entered a cloister
You're embarrassed to catch yourself mouthing
    a prayer
You laugh at yourself and your laughter sparkles
    like hellfire
The sparks of your laughter make life's dregs glitter
It's a painting hung in museum darkness
And sometimes you go to see it up close

Today you walk in Paris the women are bloody
This was I wish I could forget this was the beginning
    of the end of beauty
From fervent flames Our Lady gazed at me
    at Chartres
The blood of your Sacred Heart washed over me
    in Montmartre
Hearing the blissful words I feel ill
My love is a sickness and shameful
This image you possess sustains you through
    insomnia and anxiety
This image stays with you always

GUILLAUME APOLLINAIRE (1880–1918)   95
TRANSLATED BY BEVERLEY BIE BRAHIC

BOULEVARD DU MONTPARNASSE

Once, in a doorway in Paris, I saw
the most beautiful couple in the world.
They were each the single most beautiful thing in the
    world.
She would have been sixteen, perhaps; he twenty.
Their skin was the same shade of black: like a shiny
    Steinway.
And they stood there like the four-legged instrument
of a passion so grand one could barely imagine them
ever working, or eating, or reading a magazine.
Even they could hardly believe it.
Her hands gripped his belt loops, as they found each
    other's eyes,
because beauty like this must be held onto,
could easily run away on the power
of his long, lean thighs; or the tiny feet of her laughter.
I thought: now I will write a poem,
set in a doorway on the Boulevard du Montparnasse,
in which the brutishness of time
rates only a mention; I will say simply
that if either one should ever love another,
a greater beauty shall not be the cause.

THE FREE UNION

My woman whose tresses are wood-fire
Whose thoughts are heat-lightning
Whose body is hour-glass
My woman whose body is otter in tiger jaws
My woman whose mouth is cockade and bouquet of
  stars of the last magnitude
Whose teeth are spoor of a white mouse on the white
  earth
Whose tongue is grated glass and amber
My woman whose tongue is stabbed Host
Whose tongue is doll that opens and shuts its eyes
Whose tongue is stone past belief
My woman whose lashes are pothooks' down-strokes
Whose brows are rim of nest of swallow
My woman whose temples are slate of roof of
  greenhouse
And fug on windows
My woman whose shoulders are champagne
And fountain frozen o'er its dolphins
My woman whose wrists are matches
My woman whose fingers are hazard and ace of hearts
Whose fingers are hay
My woman whose armpits are beechmast and marten
And Midsummer Night
And privet and nest of

97

Whose arms are foam of sea and lock
And corn and mill mixed
My woman whose legs are spindles moving
In gestures of clockwork and despair
My woman whose calves are pith of elder
Whose feet are bunch of keys whose feet are caulkers
    drinking
My woman whose neck is impearled barley
My woman whose throat is golden Vale
And tryst in the bed yea the bed of the torrent
Whose breasts are night
My woman whose breasts are salt sea molehill
My woman whose breasts are crucible of ruby
Whose breasts are spectrum of rose through dew
My woman whose belly is fan of the days unfurling
Whose belly is giant claw
My woman whose back is bird soaring plumb
Whose back is quick-silver
Whose back is brightness
Whose nape is rolled stone and moist chalk
And fall of the glass that held the wine
My woman whose hips are skiff
Whose hips are candelabrum whose hips are arrow-
    feather
And stem of feather of white peacock
And numb balance
My woman whose rumps are sandstone and amianth

My woman whose rumps are shoulders of swan
My woman whose rumps are spring-time
Whose sex is iris
My woman whose sex is placer and ornithorynchus
My woman whose sex is mirror
My woman whose eyes full of tears
Whose eyes are compass needle are violet panoply
My woman whose eyes are savanna
My woman whose eyes are water to drink in prison
My woman whose eyes are wood under the axe for
    ever
Whose eyes are level of water level of air earth and
    fire

THE EARTH IS BLUE LIKE AN ORANGE

The earth is blue like an orange
Never an error words do not lie
They no longer supply what to sing with
It's up to kisses to get along
Mad ones and lovers
She her wedding mouth
All secrets all smiles
And what indulgent clothing
She looks quite naked.

The wasps are flowering green
Dawn is placing around its neck
A necklace of windows
Wings cover up the leaves
You have all the solar joys
All sunshine on the earth
On the paths of your loveliness.

TRANSLATED BY MARY ANN CAWS

PARIS AT NIGHT

Three matches one by one lit in the night
The first to see your face complete
The second one to see your eyes
The last to see your lips
And then
Darkness complete to let me think of them again
As my arms hold you hug you tight.

THE GARDEN

Thousands and thousands of years would be
Too few to tell
Sufficiently
The little second of eternity
When you kissed me
When I kissed you
When we embraced each other too
One morning in the winter light
In Paris in Parc Montsouris
Paris
A place on earth
On earth
That star in space.

IMMENSE AND RED

Immense and red
Above the Grand Palais
The winter sun appears
And disappears
Like him my heart will disappear
And all my blood will be going off
Off to look for you
My love
My beauty
And to find you too
Wherever you are.

THE MIRABEAU BRIDGE
Le Pont Mirabeau

Under the Mirabeau Bridge the Seine
      Flows and our love
   Must I be reminded again
How joy came always after pain

  Night comes the hour is rung
  The days go I remain

Hands within hands we stand face to face
      While underneath
    The bridge of our arms passes
The loose wave of our gazing which is endless

  Night comes the hour is rung
  The days go I remain

Love slips away like this water flowing
      Love slips away
   How slow life is in its going
And hope is so violent a thing

  Night comes the hour is rung
  The days go I remain

The days pass the weeks pass and are gone
Neither time that is gone
Nor love ever returns again
Under the Mirabeau Bridge flows the Seine

Night comes the hour is rung
The days go I remain

IL BACIO

Kiss! Hollyhock in the garden of caresses!
Lively accompaniment on the keyboard of the teeth
To the soft refrains that Love sings in passionate
    hearts with
Its archangel's voice to enchanting languidness!

Resonant and graceful Kiss, heavenly Kiss!
Nonpareil voluptuousness, intoxication indescribable!
All hail! The man, bent over your adorable
Cup, gets drunk there with an inexhaustible
    happiness.

As by music, as by a Rhine wine,
You cradle us and we are consoled,
And sorrow expires with a pout in your crimson
    fold ...
Let a greater one, Goethe or Will, write you a classic
    line.

Me, I can't do it, this bouquet of childish strophes
Is all I can offer, a sickly trouvère of Paris:
Be kind and, to reward me, come down on the
    mischievous
Lips of One I know, Kiss, and laugh.

PAUL VERLAINE (1844–96)

TRANSLATED BY KARL KIRCHWEY

From *A SONG OF LOVE*

Around your house I prowl without the slightest
    hope.
My sad whip hangs from my neck. And yet I observe
Through the shutters your beautiful eyes, these
    bowers,
These palaces of leaves where evening will soon die.

Whistle hustler tunes, walk with looks ready to kill,
Your heel crushing nests among the reeds, whip the
    sky
And in the shape of golden seashells in the wind
High above cut out the morning air of April,

But see it doesn't sink and lose leaves at your feet,
O you are my true strength, the most delicate star
Of the nights, between lace and snow of these islands
Your gold shoulders, white fingers of the almondtree.

106 JEAN GENET (1910–86)
TRANSLATED BY STEVEN FINCH

I WANT TO SLEEP WITH YOU

I want to sleep with you side by side
Our hair intertwined
Our sexes joined
With your mouth for a pillow.
I want to sleep with you back to back
With no breath to part us
No words to distract us
No eyes to lie to us
With no clothes on.
To sleep with you breast to breast
Tense and sweating
Shining with a thousand quivers
Consumed by ecstatic mad inertia
Stretched out on your shadow
Hammered by your tongue
To die in a rabbit's rotting teeth
Happy.

JOYCE MANSOUR (1928–86)   107
TRANSLATED BY MARY ANN CAWS

"O SO DEAR FROM FAR AWAY, SO NEAR AND WHITE ..."

O so dear from far away, so near and white, so
Deliciously you, Mary, lead me in dream where
    thrives
A balm so elusive distilled where it revives
On any flower-vase of crystal in shadow.

You know it, yes, for me, here still, as years ago,
Always your blinding smile extenuating contrives
The same rose with its fair Summer that dives
Into lost times and then into the future also.

My heart that in the nights seeks to know itself
    sometimes
And to call you with what last word most tenderly
    chimes
Bears nothing in your homage save what a sister
    sighed

Were it not, great treasure and diminutive head,
That you teach me quite otherwise a sudden delight
Softly by the sole kiss in your hair said.

108 STÉPHANE MALLARMÉ (1842–98)
TRANSLATED BY VERNON WATKINS

LADY LOVE

She is standing on my lids
And her hair is in my hair
She has the colour of my eye
She has the body of my hand
In my shade she is engulfed
As a stone against the sky

She will never close her eyes
And she does not let me sleep
And her dreams in the bright day
Make the suns evaporate
And me laugh cry and laugh
Speak when I have nothing to say

PAUL ÉLUARD (1895–1952)   109
TRANSLATED BY SAMUEL BECKETT

COLETTE

My mother used to say, "Sit down, dear,
and don't cry. The worst thing for a woman
is her first man – the one who kills you.
After that, marriage becomes a long career."
Poor Sido! She never had another career
and she knew first-hand how love ruins you.
The seducer doesn't care about his woman,
even as he whispers endearments in her ear.

Never let anyone destroy your inner spirit.
Among all the forms of truly absurd courage
the recklessness of young girls is outstanding.
Otherwise there would be far fewer marriages
and even fewer affairs that overwhelm marriages.
Look at me: it's amazing I'm still standing
after what I went through with ridiculous courage.
I was made to suffer, but no one broke my spirit.

Every woman wants her adventure to be a feast
of ripening cherries and peaches, Marseilles figs,
hot-house grapes, champagne shuddering in crystal.
Happiness, we believe, is on sumptuous display.
But unhappiness writes a different kind of play.
The gypsy gazes down into a clear blue crystal
and sees rotten cherries and withered figs.
Trust me: loneliness, too, can be a feast.

Ardor is delicious, but keep your own room.
One of my husbands said: is it impossible
for you to write a book that isn't about love,
adultery, semi-incestuous relations, separation?
(Of course, this was before our own separation.)
He never understood the natural law of love,
the arc from the possible to the impossible . . .
I have extolled the tragedy of the bedroom.

We need exact descriptions of the first passion,
so pay attention to whatever happens to you.
Observe everything: love is greedy and forgetful.
By all means fling yourself wildly into life
(though sometimes you will be flung back by life)
but don't let experience make you forgetful
and be surprised by everything that happens to you.
We are creative creatures fuelled by passion.

One final thought about the nature of love.
Freedom should be the first condition of love
and work is liberating (*a novel about love
cannot be written while you are making love*).
Never underestimate the mysteries of love,
the eminent dignity of not talking about love.
Passionate attention is prayer, prayer is love.
Savor the world. Consume the feast with love.

EDWARD HIRSCH (1950–)   111

HÔTEL SAINT GERMAIN

An expectant suitcase
A flutter of birds
Rising
A rush of flowers
Opening
Grey silk drapes
Swish
Pale thin blue spread
Ruffled
A blur of sun after rain
The pane outside
Clouds moving like music
Carried through time
The lattice
Breath like wine
How brief
His palm closing the door
Drawing closer
The gold clock with its lies
Sweet love opening like a prayer
No. It was not me. It was her. I was not there.

IN PARIS WITH YOU

Don't talk to me of love. I've had an earful
And I get tearful when I've downed a drink or two.
I'm one of your talking wounded.
I'm a hostage. I'm maroonded.
But I'm in Paris with you.

Yes I'm angry at the way I've been bamboozled
And resentful at the mess I've been through.
I admit I'm on the rebound
And I don't care where are we bound.
I'm in Paris with you.

Do you mind if we do not go to the Louvre
If we say sod off to sodding Notre Dame,
If we skip the Champs Elysées
And remain here in this sleazy

Old hotel room
Doing this and that
To what and whom
Learning who you are,
Learning what I am.

Don't talk to me of love. Let's talk of Paris,
The little bit of Paris in our view.

There's that crack across the ceiling
And the hotel walls are peeling
And I'm in Paris with you.

Don't talk to me of love. Let's talk of Paris.
I'm in Paris with the slightest thing you do.
I'm in Paris with your eyes, your mouth,
I'm in Paris with ... all points south.
Am I embarrassing you?
I'm in Paris with you.

EXPATRIATES

BLACK STONE LYING ON A
WHITE STONE

I will die in Paris, on a rainy day,
on some day I can already remember.
I will die in Paris – and I don't step aside –
perhaps on a Thursday, as today is Thursday,
    in autumn.

It will be a Thursday, because today, Thursday,
    setting down
these lines, I have put my upper arm bones on
wrong, and never so much as today have I found
    myself
with all the road ahead of me, alone.

César Vallejo is dead. Everyone beat him
although he never does anything to them;
they beat him hard with a stick and hard also

with a rope. These are the witnesses:
the Thursdays, and the bones of my arms,
the solitude, and the rain, and the roads . . .

CÉSAR VALLEJO (1892–1938)   117
TRANSLATED BY ROBERT BLY

IN PARIS

Roofs reach the stars, the sky is low,
And closer to the earth, its vapours thronging
In Paris, so large, so full of joy,
Still the old secret longing.

The evening boulevards hum and throb
The last light of dusk dies.
Everywhere couples, couples in love,
Trembling lips and brazen eyes.

I'm alone here. How sweet
To lean my head on a chestnut's bole
And hear in my heart Rostand weep
As he did once before, in Moscow.

Paris at night is strange and piteous –
Dearer to my heart is the fevered past
I go home, to the violets' dreariness
And a tender face behind picture glass.

That gaze – companion to my sorrow
That fond profile on the wall,
Rostand, and Reichstadt, his poor hero
And Sarah, at night they visit me, all.

In Paris, so large, so full of joy
I see grass, I see high clouds in my sleep
And laughter far off, and shadows close by
And the pain is always just as deep.

MARINA TSVETAEVA (1892–1941)   119
TRANSLATED BY SASHA DUGDALE

GOODBYE TO PARIS

How beautiful the Seine, abundant river
with its cindery trees,
with its towers and its spires.

And what have I come to do here?

Everything more elegant than a rose,
a tousled rose,
a languishing rose.
This place is crepuscular.
Twilight and dawn
are two river boats,
and they pass and repass,
making no sign, indifferent,
having known and loved each other
for a thousand thousand years.

For almost too much time.

The stone wizened and
the yellow cathedrals grew,
the extravagant power stations,
and now autumn consumes the sky,
feeds on clouds and smoke,
sets up like a black king
at the smoky water's edge.

There is no afternoon sweeter in the world.
Everything settling at the same time,
the blunt colour, the vague cry,
only the mist remains
and the light wrapped in the trees
putting on its green dress.

I have so much to do in Chile.
Salinas and Laura are waiting,
to everyone in my country I owe something,
and at this moment the table is set
for me in every house;
others lie in wait to wound me,
but besides there are those trees
with metallic foliage
which know my unhappiness,
my joy, my miseries,
those wings are my wings,
that is the water I love,
the sea as heavy as stone,
vaster than those buildings,
hard and blue like a star.

And what have I come to do here?

How did I arrive in these parts?

I have to be where they call me
to baptize the cement,
to mix sand and men,
touch shovels and earth,
for we must do everything
there on our born ground;
we have to found a country,
song, bread and delight,
our honour has to be clean
as a queen's fingernails
and our purified flags
so will float in the wind
over the crystalline towers.

Goodbye, Paris and autumn,
blue ship, amorous sea,
goodbye rivers, bridges, goodbye
crackling, fragrant bread,
deep suave wine, goodbye
and goodbye, friends who loved me,
I go singing across seas
and I go back to breathe my roots.
My address is vague, I live
on the high seas and on high land.
My city is geography.
The street is called "I Go",
the number, "Not to Return".

TRANSLATED BY ALASTAIR REID

From *HAIKU, THIS OTHER WORLD*

41
Just before dawn,
When the streets are deserted,
A light spring rain.

415
In a drizzling rain,
In a flower shop's doorway,
A girl sells herself.

574
Standing in the crowd
In a cold drizzling rain, –
How lonely it is.

From HÔTEL FRANÇOIS 1ER

It was a very little while and they had gone in front of it. It was that they had liked it would it bear. It was a very much adjoined a follower. Flower of an adding where a follower.

Have I come in. Will in suggestion.

They may like hours in catching.

It is always a pleasure to remember.

Have a habit.

Any name will very well wear better.

All who live round about there.

Have a manner.

The hôtel François 1er.

Just winter so.

It is indubitably often that she is as denied to soften help to when it is in all in midst of which in vehemence to taken given in a bestowal show than left help in double.

Having noticed often that it is newly noticed which makes older often.

The world has become smaller and more beautiful.

The world is grown smaller and more beautiful.

That is it.

Yes that is it.

If he liked to live elsewhere that was natural.

If he was accompanied.

Place praise places.
But you do.
Partly for you.
Will he he wild in having a room soon. He was not
very welcome. Safety in their choice.
Amy whether they thought much of merry. I do
marry del Val.
I know how many do walk too.
It was a while that they did wait for them to have an
apple.
An apple.
She may do this for the Hôtel Lion d'Or.

II

Buy me yesterday for they may adhere to coffee.
It is without doubt no pleasure to walk about.

III

The romance of the Hôtel François premier is this
that it was seen on a Saturday.

From LETTER TO F. SCOTT FITZGERALD

Was it fun in Paris? Who did you see there and was the Madeleine pink at five o'clock and did the fountains fall with hollow delicacy into the framing of space in the Place de la Concorde, and did the blue creep out from behind the Colonades of the rue de Rivoli through the grill of the Tuileries and was the Louvre gray and metallic in the sun and did the trees hang brooding over the cafés and were there lights at night and the click of saucers and the auto horns that play de Bussey –

I *love* Paris. How was it?

Late summer/early fall 1930

Prangins Clinc,
Nyon, Switzerland

MONTPARNASSE

There are never any suicides in the quarter among
    people one knows
No successful suicides.
A Chinese boy kills himself and is dead.
(they continue to place his mail in the letter rack at the
    Dome)
A Norwegian boy kills himself and is dead.
(no one knows where the other Norwegian boy has
    gone)
They find a model dead
alone in bed and very dead.
(it made almost unbearable trouble for the concierge)
Sweet oil, the white of eggs, mustard and water, soap
    suds
and stomach pumps rescue the people one knows.
Every afternoon the people one knows can be found at
    the café.

ERNEST HEMINGWAY (1899–1961)   127

From THE PARIS POEM

Wondrous at night is gaunt Paris.
Hark! Under the vaults of black arcades,
where the walls are rocklike, the urinals
gurgle behind their shields.

There is Fate and an alpine something
in that desolate splash. Any moment now,
between even and odd, between me and non-me,
that keeper of records will choke and drown.

And the bridges! That's bliss everlasting,
the bliss of black water. Look, what a sight:
the vitrine of an incomparable pharmacy
and the globes of lamps full of orange light.

Overhead – matters there are less pretty.
Without end. Without end. Just a mist.
A dead moon phantasmed in its millpool.
Can it be that I too—? Dismissed.

Death is distant yet (after tomorrow
I'll think everything through); but now and then
one's heart starts clamoring: Author! Author!
He is not in the house, gentlemen.

And while I looked at the crescent
as blue as a bruise, there came
from a distant suburb, the whistle
– heartrending sound! – of a train.

A huge clean sheet of paper I started
to extract from myself. The sheet
was bigger than me and frenetically
it rolled up in a funnel and creaked.

And the struggle began to seem muddled,
unresolvable: I, the black sky,
I, the lights, and the present minute –
and the present minute went by.

But who knows – perhaps, it was priceless
and perhaps I'd regret some day
having treated that sheet of paper
in such an inhuman way.

Perhaps something to me they incanted –
those stones and that whistle afar?
And on the sidewalk groping, my crumpled
scrap of paper I found in the dark.

VLADIMIR NABOKOV (1899–1977)   129
TRANSLATED BY DMITRI NABOKOV

IN MEMORIAM

Today is Sunday.
I fear the crowd of my fellows with such faces of stone.
From my glass tower filled with headaches and
    impatient Ancestors,
I contemplate the roofs and hilltops in the mist.
In the stillness – somber, naked chimneys.
Below them my dead are asleep and my dreams turn
    to ashes.
All my dreams, blood running freely down the streets
And mixing with blood from the butcher shops.
From this observatory like the outskirts of town
I contemplate my dreams lost along the streets,
Crouched at the foot of the hills like the guides of my
    race
On the rivers of the Gambia and the Saloum
And now on the Seine at the foot of these hills.
Let me remember my dead!
Yesterday was All Saints' Day, the solemn anniversary
    of the Sun,
And I had no dead to honor in any cemetery.
O Forefathers! You who have always refused to die,
Who knew how to resist Death from the Sine to the
    Seine,
And now in the fragile veins of my indomitable blood,

Guard my dreams as you did your thin-legged
    migrant sons!
O Ancestors! Defend the roofs of Paris in this
    dominical fog,
The roofs that protect my dead.
Let me leave this tower so dangerously secure
And descend to the streets, joining my brothers
Who have blue eyes and hard hands.

LÉOPOLD SÉDAR SENGHOR (1906–2001)   131
TRANSLATED BY MELVIN DIXON

"YOU DON'T KNOW NIGHTS OF LOVE?"

You don't know nights of love? Don't
petals of soft words float upon your blood?
Are there no places on your dear body
that keep remembering like eyes?

Paris, summer 1909

LE DÔME
Montparnasse

This keepsake you've bequeathed me, a face among
    mirrors and dirty saucers,
contributes to my suspicion that the universe
  isn't perfect.
The awkwardness of our last hour together
argues the certainty that the sun is poisoned,
that inside every grain of wheat a deadly weapon
    trembles,
when it all should have come clear, in a silence
where nothing would have been left unsaid.
But that's not how it was, and we parted
the way we deserved to, really, in a
    filthy café,
surrounded by ghosts and cigarette butts,
mixing our pitiful kisses with night's undertow.

JULIO CORTÁZAR (1914–84)   133
TRANSLATED BY STEPHEN KESSLER

SANIES II

there was a happy land
the American Bar
in Rue Mouffetard
there were red eggs there
I have a dirty I say henorrhoids
coming from the bath
the steam the delight the sherbet
the chagrin of the old skinnymalinks
slouching happy body
loose in my stinking old suit
sailing slouching up to Puvis the gauntlet of tulips
lash lash me with yaller tulips I will let down
my stinking old trousers
my love she sewed up the pockets alive the live-oh she
    did she said that was better
spotless then within the brown rags gliding
frescoward free up the fjord of dyed eggs and
    thongbells
I disappear don't you know into the local
the mackerel are at billiards there they are crying the
    scores
the Barfrau makes a big impression with her mighty
    bottom
Dante and blissful Beatrice are there
prior to Vita Nuova

the balls splash no luck comrade
Gracieuse is there Belle-Belle down the drain
booted Percinet with his cobalt jowl
they are necking gobble-gobble
suck is not suck that alters
lo Alighieri has got off au revoir to all that
I break down quite in a titter of despite
hark
upon the saloon a terrible hush
a shiver convulses Madame de la Motte
it courses it peals down her collops
the great bottom foams into stillness
quick quick the cavaletto supplejacks for mumbo-
     jumbo
vivas puellas mortui incurrrrrsant boves
oh subito subito ere she recover the cang bamboo for
     bastinado
a bitter moon fessade à la mode
oh Becky spare me I have done thee no wrong spare
     me damn thee
spare me good Becky
call off thine adders Becky I will compensate thee
     in full
Lord have mercy upon
Christ have mercy upon us

Lord have mercy upon us

SAMUEL BECKETT (1906–89)

From MON PÈRE, ELEGY FOR
PAUL CELAN*

Hanging on by a hair,
on that night different
from all other nights,
he could not pull himself out
by a breath.
He was something like hair
with feeling only at its roots.
Coming from a musical family,
he could not bear to hear music,
he could not stop
his constant, endless bleeding
in private, in public,
on the bread he ate,
on my mother's face.
Drowning
sent his life and blood off
in water like smoke.
His fingers were dactyls again.

A fisherman found him
decomposing black below
Notre Dame Cathedral,
where in the Chapel of Virtues
the Virgin wept for her son

surrounded by images
of women without lives:
Temperance, Fortitude, Justice,
and Prudence with her three eyes
to see past, present and future.

Once his garments were warmed
when Jehovah quieted the earth
with the south wind.

The language of the psalms
has a different word
for why asked in the past
and why asked in the future.
Why lose the rest of spring, mon père?

* The poet Paul Celan threw himself into the Seine, April 21, 1970
(the first night of Passover). His son is an aerialist and juggler.

STANLEY MOSS (1925–)   137

"BEFORE THE TIME RUNS OUT, MY ROSE"

Before the time runs out, my rose,
before Paris is burned down and destroyed,
before the time runs out, my rose,
and my heart is still on its branch,
I, one night, one of these May nights,
holding you against the wall in Quai Voltaire,
must kiss you on the lips
then turning our faces toward Notre Dame
we must gaze at its rose window
my rose, suddenly you must embrace me,
with fear, surprise and happiness,
sobbing silently,
the stars too must pour
mixed with a drizzling rain.
Before the time runs out, my rose,
before Paris is burned down and destroyed,
before the time runs out, my rose,
and my heart is still on its branch,
in this night of May
we must pass by the quay
        under the willows, my rose,
the weeping willows that are drenched.

I must tell you the most beautiful couple of words
     of Paris,
          the loveliest and truest,
then whistling some airs
I must die of happiness
          and we must have faith in human beings.

Up there stone houses
without ledges or recesses
stuck together
and their walls are all moonlight
and their windows straight up
          are sleeping standing up
and on the shore across the Louvre
bathed in floodlights
our crystal palace
illuminated for us.

Before the time runs out, my rose,
before Paris is burned and destroyed,
before the time runs out, my rose,
and my heart is still on its branch,
in this night of May on the quay we must sit
on the red barrels in front of the warehouses.

The canal across fades into darkness.
A barge is passing,
my rose, let's say hello,
let's say hello to the barge with the yellow cabin.
Is she on her way to Belgium or to Holland?
In the cabin door a woman with a white apron
          is smiling sweetly.

Before the time runs out, my rose,
before Paris is burned down and destroyed,
before the time runs out, my rose ...
People of Paris, people of Paris,
You mustn't let Paris be burned and destroyed ...

TRANSLATED BY NILÜFER MIZANOĞLU REDDY

TOURISTS

AT PÈRE LACHAISE

What began as death's avenue
becomes, as we go on,
death's village, then metropolis,
and the four of us,
reading our rain-blistered Michelin
map of graves, keep looking back,
but cafés, tabacs,
boulangeries are gone.
It is a long way yet
to where we are going to please me,
and the bunch of muguets
I am holding too tightly is frayed
already. On either side
of the cobbles we slip on,
darkly arched over by dripping chestnuts,
the ten foot high deathhouses
stand, and we can see
at hilltop intersections
only further suburbs of
the imposing dead.
For a while we are lost
in this silent city –
the map is not detailed
and the avenues curve.
It is cold here. I am very cold.

My friend begins to cry.
We find a Kleenex for her
and a tranquilizer.
Head bent, hand clenched
to her mouth, her black bob
spattered with chestnut petals,
she stumbles and turns her ankle.
I am to blame.
A whole afternoon in Paris spent
on this spooky pilgrimage,
and we are too far in to go back.
The rain has stopped.
"Look, my God, *look!*"
Anything awful can happen here,
but I look where she points.
Ahead, at a break in the trees
where a weak ray of sun shines through,
two of the great dun tombs
are dappled with color, with cats,
more cats than I can believe,
two dozen at least,
sitting or lying on doorsills,
window ledges, pedestals, roofs,
and a yellow one, high in the air,
curled round at rest on the bar
of a towering cross.
Grimalkins, grandpas,

lithe rakes, plump dowagers,
princes, peasants, old warriors, hoydens,
gray, white, black, cream, orange,
spotted, striped and plain –
a complete society of cats,
posed while we stand and stare.
My heart is thumping.
"Are we dreaming?
Oh, aren't they beautiful!"
my friend whispers.
We smile at the cats for a long time
before we go on past.
We are almost there.

Off to the side,
behind the grand monuments,
we find a flat slab marked MARCEL PROUST
and, feeling a little foolish,
I lay my fistsized white bouquet
on his black marble.
We go back another way
where the street widens,
opening out to gardens,
and we run down broad steps,
laughing at nothing.
A few people appear,
arranging gladioli in urns,

and far down the hill we can see
an exit to the boulevard.
We find Colette's grave
on the way out and call to her,
"You should have seen the cats!"

PARIS SYNDROME

The Eiffel Tower erected itself in my head,
we couldn't find the lifts, climbed the stairs.

Of course there were fireworks.

We stared at each other, rare exhibits in the Louvre –
you licked my *Mona Lisa* smile right off.

Of course we were both in imaginary Chanel.

We drank warm cider and ate pancakes, yours
    flambéed.
I got drunk, my tights laddered on both legs.

Of course we experienced tachycardia at the Moulin
    Rouge.

Our hotel, a boxed macaron on a navy boulevard –
we spun around in the dark outside, rain-dizzy.

Of course we slept at the Ritz.

Our little room tucked into the corner, a pink
pocket you slipped into that night.

Of course our fingers hunted for change.

In the mirrored elevator I couldn't meet your eye, I
crushed you into the laminated sample menu and died.

Of course it was only *la petite mort*.

PLAN DU CENTRE DE PARIS
À VOL D'OISEAU

Flying away to Milan
I look down and back at Paris
(as in that famous map
seen by a bird in flight)
and think of Allen yesterday
saying it was all "solidified nostalgia" –
houses monuments and streets
bare trees and parks down there
fixed in time (and the time is forever)
exactly where we left them years ago
our bodies passed through them
as through a transparent scrim
Early versions of ourselves
transmuted now
two decades later
And was that myself
standing on that far corner
Place Saint-Sulpice
first arrived in Paris –
seabag slung –
(fancying myself some seaborn Conrad
carrying Coleridge's albatross?)
or was that myself walking
through the Tuileries in snow?

And here Danton met Robespierre
(both later to descend into earth
through that Métro entrance)
And here Sartre lived with Beauvoir
above the Café Bonaparte
before death
shook them apart
(The myth goes on)
And here in the Luxembourg
I sat by a balustrade
in a rented iron chair
reading Proust and Apollinaire
while the day turned to dust
and a nightwood sprang up around me
Solidified nostalgia indeed –
the smell of Gaulois still hangs in the air
And in the cemetery of Père Lachaise
the great stone tombs still yawn
with the solidified ennui of eternity
And, yes, here I knew such aloneness –
at the corner of another street
the dawn yawned
in some trauma I was living in back then
Paris itself a floating dream
a great stone ship adrift
made of dusk and dawn and darkness –

dumb trauma
of youth!
such wastes of love
such wordless hungers
mute neuroses
yearnings & gropings
fantasies & flame-outs
such endless walking
through the bent streets
such fumbling art
(models drawn with blindfolds)
such highs and sweet inebriations –
I salute you now
dumb inchoate youth
(callow stripling!)
and offer you my left hand
with a slight derisive laugh

A FIRST DAY IN PARIS

Some twenty years ago I was still a young man. I did not know anything more about Paris than a small black-haired sea tern knows about inland mountain gardens on the first day of his life. All he does is gaze around him, puzzled at the solitary distances of the ocean. How many mountains I have flown across, how many nests I have lain down in and abandoned between the big American cities. Now I walk in the gardens of the Tuileries. Here, a song tells me, some twenty years ago the chestnut buds in April were too heavy to bear themselves any longer. When a late frost fell on them, they suddenly shuddered in the night, and the next morning they opened, green as before, in spite of everything. The startled frost ran off and vanished, and the open blossoms turned white in their own good time. In Paris the natural world, alert and welcome in a moment to its own loveliness, offers a strange new face, as though God were creating it for the first time. Sometimes the women in the Tuileries grow so old they outlive death, and their shadows lie on chestnut leaves like sunlight.

TO THE FRENCH LANGUAGE

I needed to find you and, once having found you,
    to keep you
You who could make me a physical Larousse
Of everyday living, you who would present me to
    Gilberte
And Anna and Sonia, you by whom I could be a
    surrealist
And a dadaist and almost a fake of Racine and of
    Molière. I was hiding
The heavenly dolor you planted in my heart:
That I would never completely have you.
I wanted to take you with me on long vacations
Always giving you so many kisses, ma française –
Across rocky mountains, valleys, and lakes
And I wanted it to be as if
Nous faisions ce voyage pour l'éternité
Et non pas uniquement pour la brève durée d'une
    année boursière en France.
Those days, and that idea, are gone.
A little hotel on the rue de Fleurus
Was bursting with you.
And one April morning, when I woke up, I had you
Stuck to the tip of my tongue like a Christmas sticker
I walked out into the street, it was Fleurus
And said hello which came out Bonjour Madame

I walked to the crémerie four doors away and sat down.
I was lifted up by you. I knew I couldn't be anything
    to you
But an aspiring lover. Sans ego. It was the best
    relationship
Of relationships sans ego, that I've ever had.
I know you love flattery and are so good at it that one
    can hardly believe
What you are saying when it is expressed in you.
But I have loved you. That's no flattering statement
But the truth. And still love you, though now I'm not
    in love with you.
The woman who first said this to me nearly broke my
    heart,
But I don't think I'm breaking yours, because it's a
    coeur
In the first place and, for another thing, it beats under
    le soleil
On a jeudi or vendredi matin and besides you're not
    listening to me
At least not as you did on the days
I sat around in Aix-en-Provence's cafés waiting for you
To spark a conversation – about nothing in particular.
    I was on stage
At all times, and you were the script and the audience
Even when the theatre had no people in it, you were
    there.

154 KENNETH KOCH (1925–2002)

TO A FRENCH STRUCTURALIST

There's no modesty, Todorov,
in the park where I read:
the young mothers and working girls
raise their skirts and open their blouses
to the sun while the children play,
the old men doze, and I wrestle
with your *Poetics.* When I look again,
perhaps they'll all be naked;
they'll make for the seesaw and jungle gym,
bosoms swinging and long legs flashing
in the midday light. Ah, that clerk
at the Préfecture de Police
looked at me with such disdain
when he asked what I was doing in Paris!
It was a lie, Todorov,
when I shrugged and said, "Nothing."

JANUARY IN PARIS

> Poems are never completed – they are
> only abandoned.
>
>   – Paul Valéry

That winter I had nothing to do
but tend the kettle in my shuttered room
on the top floor of a pensione near a cemetery,

but I would sometimes descend the stairs,
unlock my bicycle, and pedal along the cold city
      streets
often turning from a wide boulevard
down a narrow side street
bearing the name of an obscure patriot.

I followed a few private rules,
never crossing a bridge without stopping
mid-point to lean my bike on the railing
and observe the flow of the river below
as I tried to better understand the French.

In my pale coat and my Basque cap
I pedaled past the windows of a patisserie
or sat up tall in the seat, arms folded,
and clicked downhill filling my nose with winter air.

I would see beggars and street cleaners
in their bright uniforms, and sometimes
I would see the poems of Valéry,
the ones he never finished but abandoned,
wandering the streets of the city half-clothed.

Most of them needed only a final line
or two, a little verbal flourish at the end,
but whenever I approached,
they would retreat from their makeshift fires
into the shadows – thin specters of incompletion,

forsaken for so many long decades
how could they ever trust another man with a pen?

I came across the one I wanted to tell you about
sitting with a glass of rosé at a café table –
beautiful, emaciated, unfinished,
cruelly abandoned with a flick of panache

by Monsieur Paul Valéry himself,
big fish in the school of Symbolism
and for a time, president of the Committee of Arts
    and Letters
of the League of Nations if you please.

Never mind how I got her out of the café,
past the concierge and up the flights of stairs –
remember that Paris is the capital of public kissing.

And never mind the holding and the pressing.
It is enough to know that I moved my pen
in such a way as to bring her to completion,

a simple, final stanza, which ended,
as this poem will, with the image
of a gorgeous orphan lying on a rumpled bed,
her large eyes closed,
a painting of cows in a valley over her head,

and off to the side, me in a window seat
blowing smoke from a cigarette at dawn.

VOCABULARY

"*La Pologne? La Pologne?* Isn't it terribly cold there?" she asked, and then sighed with relief. So many countries have been turning up lately that the safest thing to talk about is climate.

"Madame," I want to reply, "my people's poets do all their writing in mittens. I don't mean to imply that they never remove them; they do, indeed, if the moon is warm enough. In stanzas composed of raucous whooping, for only such can drown the windstorms' constant roar, they glorify the simple lives of our walrus herders. Our Classicists engrave their odes with inky icicles on trampled snowdrifts. The rest, our Decadents, bewail their fate with snowflakes instead of tears. He who wishes to drown himself must have an ax at hand to cut the ice. Oh, madame, dearest madame."

That's what I mean to say. But I've forgotten the word for walrus in French. And I'm not sure of icicle and ax.

"*La Pologne? La Pologne?* Isn't it terribly cold there?"

"*Pas du tout,*" I answer icily.

WISLAWA SZYMBORSKA (1923–2012)   159
TRANSLATED BY CLARE CAVANAGH AND
STANISLAW BARAŃCZAK

NO ONE GOES TO PARIS IN AUGUST

A Montparnasse August
with view of the Cimetière. A yard of bones.

We wake to it. Close curtains to it.
Wake to its lanes. Rows of coffin-stones in varying
    light.

Walking here. Late with shade low, low, long.
We're passing through, just passing through
neat aisles of gray mausoleums.

(From Paris. Send this postcard. This one.
Calm water lilies. Water lilies.
Nothing colorless.)

It's morning. Baudelaire's tomb.
Tree limbs casting shadow west.

This, a lot of time under a looming sky.
Nobody has time like this.
(Time to go to Le Mandarin for coffee
every day. We're not complaining.
They bring the milk separate.
Watch the passersby on Saint-Germain.)

Nothing to ponder. This is the plight.
Pause by Pigeon in bed with his wife –
both fully dressed.

Pink flowers, pink flowers,
just beneath de Beauvoir's name.
When she lived she lived two doors down.
Went south in August.

All of us smell of heat all the time.
We are the living. Oh dear!
There are the dead ones there.
Their thoughts more familiar, though.
Lives finished, nearly clear.
And they make it possible for us to go on living
as we do in their blue shade.

FOOD AND DRINK

From *FLORIO*

'Twas sauce! 'twas sweetmeat! 'twas confection!
All poignancy! and all perfection!
Rich *entremets,* whose name none knows,
Ragouts, tourtes, tendrons, fricandeaux,
Might picque the sensuality
O' th' hogs of Epicurus' sty;
Yet all so foreign, and so fine,
'Twas easier to admire than dine.

O! if the muse had power to tell
Each dish, no muse has power to spell!
Great goddess of the French *cuisine*!
Not with unhallow'd hands I mean
To violate thy secret shade,
Which eyes profane shall ne'er invade;
No! of thy dignity supreme,
I, with "mysterious reverence," deem!
Or should I venture with rash hand,
The vulgar would not understand;
None but th' initiated know
The raptures keen thy rites bestow.

HANNAH MORE (1745–1833)   165

LES BOULANGERS

Blessed be the breadmakers of la belle France
who rise before dawn to plunge their arms
into great tubs of dough. Blessed be the yeast
and its amazing redoubling. Praise the nimble
tongues of those who gave names to this plenty:
baguette, boule, brioche, ficelle, pain de campagne.
Praise the company they keep, their fancier cousins:
croissant, mille feuille, chausson aux pommes.
Praise flake after golden flake. Bless their saintly
counterparts: *Jésuit, religieuse, sacristain, pets de nonne.*
Praise be to the grain, and the men who grew it. Bless
the rising up, and the punching down. The great
elasticity. The crust and the crumb. Bless
the butter sighing as it melts in the heat.
The smear of confiture that gilds the plane.
And bless us, too, O my brothers,
for we have sinned, and we are truly hungry.

From THE BALLAD OF BOUILLABAISSE

A street there is in Paris famous,
    For which no rhyme our language yields,
Rue Neuve des petits Champs its name is –
    The New Street of the Little Fields;
And there's an inn, not rich and splendid,
    But still in comfortable case –
The which in youth I oft attended,
    To eat a bowl of Bouillabaisse.

This Bouillabaisse a noble dish is –
    A sort of soup, or broth, or brew,
Or hotchpotch of all sorts of fishes,
    That Greenwich never could outdo;
Green herbs, red peppers, mussels, saffern,
    Soles, onions, garlic, roach, and dace;
All these you eat at Terré's tavern,
    In that one dish of Bouillabaisse.

Indeed, a rich and savory stew 't is;
    And true philosophers, methinks,
Who love all sorts of natural beauties,
    Should love good victuals and good drinks.
And Cordelier or Benedictine
    Might gladly, sure, his lot embrace,
Nor find a fast-day too afflicting,
    Which served him up a Bouillabaisse.

I wonder if the house still there is?
    Yes, here the lamp is as before;
The smiling, red-cheeked écaillère is
    Still opening oysters at the door.
Is Terré still alive and able?
    I recollect his droll grimace;
He'd come and smile before your table,
    And hop'd you lik'd your Bouillabaisse.

We enter; nothing's changed or older.
    "How's Monsieur Terré, waiter, pray?"
The waiter stares and shrugs his shoulder; –
    "Monsieur is dead this many a day."
"It is the lot of saint and sinner.
    So honest Terré's run his race!"
"What will Monsieur require for dinner?"
    "Say, do you still cook Bouillabaisse?"

"Oh, oui, Monsieur,"'s the waiter's answer;
    "Quel vin Monsieur désire-t-il?"
"Tell me a good one." "That I can, sir;
    The Chambertin with yellow seal."
"So Terré's gone," I say and sink in
    My old accustom'd corner-place;
"He's done with feasting and with drinking,
    With Burgundy and Bouillabaisse."

BE DRUNK

You have to be always drunk. That's all there is to it –
it's the only way. So as not to feel the horrible burden
of time that breaks your back and bends you to the
earth, you have to be continually drunk.

But on what? Wine, poetry or virtue, as you wish. But
be drunk.

And if sometimes, on the steps of a palace or the green
grass of a ditch, in the mournful solitude of your room,
you wake again, drunkenness already diminishing or
gone, ask the wind, the wave, the star, the bird, the
clock, everything that is flying, everything that is
groaning, everything that is rolling, everything that is
singing, everything that is speaking ... ask what time
it is and wind, wave, star, bird, clock will answer you:
"It is time to be drunk! So as not to be the martyred
slaves of time, be drunk, be continually drunk! On
wine, on poetry or on virtue as you wish."

CHARLES BAUDELAIRE (1821–67)   169
TRANSLATED BY LOUIS SIMPSON

WINE

The flowers I planted along my road
Have lasted long despite winds and cold
Already fiery noons begin to burn
Slyly the secret of the roots
And I know that of my footsteps nothing will remain
But a trace a cluster a drop
To recall along the paths I've chosen
Those evenings when the light sang
In eyes hands hearts and goblets.

I love the sweet harshness on the tongue
Filling the palate with a promised saliva
Knocking the mute keyboard of the teeth
With raised draperies of which one might say
That memory retains a fleeting trail of them
Half-glimpsed we won't know how or else
The loud reminder of the single moment
All gravity banished the unconscious pleasure
  recaptured
Of being nothing but entirely animal.

For our life closed on that iridescent sphere
– Color taste perfume at their extreme limits – invokes
Some miracle independent of its origin
Produced by distilling air and earth –

Like the move toward technological planets
After a calculation made on the fingers of one hand –
Time contained flowing – continual autumn
This evening this wine that enters me to make
My head light my tongue loose my cock happy.

PIERRE MARTORY (1920–98)   171
TRANSLATED BY JOHN ASHBERY

VERLAINE DRINKS

There will always be whores on street corners,
Lost shells stranded on the stellar shores
Of a blue dusk which is neither of here nor of earth
Where taxis roll by like bewildered bugs.

But roll less than in my whirling head
The green gem of absinthe deep in the glass
Where I drink perdition and the thunder
Of the Lord's judgment to roast my naked soul.

Ah! how the tangled spindles of the streets
Turn and spin the fabric of men and women,
As if a spider were weaving her web
With the filaments of discovered souls.

TRANSLATED BY HELEN WEAVER

THE SOUL OF THE WINE

sang by night in its bottles: "Dear mankind –
dear and disinherited! Break the seal
of scarlet wax that darkens my glass jail,
and I shall bring you light and brotherhood!

How long you labored on the fiery hills
among the needful vines! I know it cost
fanatic toil to make me what I am,
and I shall not be thankless or malign:

I take a potent pleasure when I pour
down the gullet of a workingman,
and how much more I relish burial
in his hot belly than in my cold vaults!

Listen to my music after hours,
the hope that quickens in my throbbing heart;
lean on the table with your sleeves rolled up
and honor me: you will know happiness,

for I shall bring a gleam to your wife's eyes,
a glow of power to your son's wan cheeks
and for this athlete flagging in the race
shall be the oil that strengthens wrestlers' limbs.

Into you I shall flow, ambrosia brewed
from precious seed the eternal Sower cast,
so that the poetry born of our love will grow
and blossom like a flower in God's sight!"

THE ARTS

POULENC

My first day in Paris I walked
            from Saint Germain to the Pont Mirabeau
in soft amber light and leaves
            and love was running out

city of light and hearts
            city of dusk and dismay
the Seine believed it to be true
            that I was unloved and alone

how lonely is that bridge
            without your song
the Avenue Mozart, the rue Pergolèse
            the tobaccos and the nuns

all Paris is alone for this
            brief leafless moment
and snow falls down upon
            the streets of our peculiar hearts

FRANK O'HARA (1926–66)   177

BOJANGLES AND JO

Stairstep music: ups,
downs, Bill Robinson smiling,
jazzdancing the rounds.

She raised champagne lips,
danced inside banana hips.
All Paris wooed   Jo.

Banana panties,
perfumed belt, Jazz tattooing
lush ecstasies felt.

Josephine, royal,
jewelling her dance, flushing
the bosom of France.

JAZZ BAND IN A
PARISIAN CABARET

Play that thing,
Jazz band!
Play it for the lords and ladies,
For the dukes and counts,
For the whores and gigolos,
For the American millionaires,
And the school teachers
Out for a spree.
Play it,
Jazz band!
You know that tune
That laughs and cries at the same time.
You know it.

   May I?
   Mais oui.
   Mein Gott!
   Parece una rumba.
Play it, jazz band!
You've got seven languages to speak in
And then some,
Even if you do come from Georgia.
   Can I go home wid yuh, sweetie?
   Sure.

CHET BAKER IN PARIS

In September of that year
when Paris had not yet turned her leaves
into pigments of dry reds and burnt umber,
you played your melodious trumpet sounds,
no mawkish phrases, no murmurings
sinking into the false twists, just cool jazz.
When all is said and done, no one
loved you more than your trumpet,
sending its small, lovely notes to the
night winds near Club St. Germain.

You played, "Those Foolish Things",
"Tenderly" and "Summertime" with sad
trumpet walks on stage at the Salle Pleyel,
your phrases clear,
soft heat in April,
everything happening to you.

TOULOUSE-LAUTREC AT THE
MOULIN ROUGE

"Cognac – more cognac for Monsieur Lautrec –
More cognac for the little gentleman,
Monster or clown of the Moulin – quick –
Another glass!"
                              The Can Can
Chorus with their jet net stockings
And their red heads rocking
Have brought their patrons flocking to the floor.
Pince-nez, glancing down from legs advancing
To five fingers dancing
Over a menu-card, scorn and adore
Prostitutes and skinny flirts
Who crossing arms and tossing skirts
High-kick – a quick
Eye captures all before they fall –
Quick lines, thick lines
Trace the huge ache under rouge.

"Cognac – more cognac!" Only the slop
Of a charwoman pushing her bucket and mop,
And the rattle of chairs on a table top.
The glass can fall no further. Time to stop
The charcoal's passionate waltzing with the hand.
Time to take up the hat, drag out the sticks,

And very slowly, like a hurt crab, stand:
With one wry bow to the vanished band,
Launch out with short steps harder than high kicks
Along the unspeakable inches of the street.
His flesh was his misfortune: but the feet
Of those whose flesh was all their fortune beat
Softly as the grey rain falling
Through his brain recalling
Marie, Annette, Jean-Claude and Marguerite.

[Musée Rodin]
RODIN'S THINKER

With his chin fallen on his rough hand,
the Thinker, remembering that his flesh is of the grave,
mortal flesh, naked before its fate,
flesh that hates death, trembled for beauty.

And he trembled for love, his whole ardent spring,
and now in autumn, he is overcome with truth and
     sadness.
"We must die" passes across his brow,
in every piercing trumpet sound, when night begins
     to fall.

And in his anguish, his long suffering muscles split.
The furrows of his flesh are filled with terrors.
It splits, like the autumn leaf before the mighty Lord

who calls it with trumpet calls ... And there is no
     tree twisted
by the sun in the plain, nor lion wounded on its side,
as tense as this man who meditates on death.

GABRIELA MISTRAL (1889–1957)   183
TRANSLATED BY GUSTAVO ALFARO

From SEURAT'S SUNDAY AFTERNOON
ALONG THE SEINE
To Meyer and Lillian Schapiro

What are they looking at? Is it the river?
The sunlight on the river, the summer, leisure,
Or the luxury and nothingness of consciousness?
A little girl skips, a ring-tailed monkey hops
Like a kangaroo, held by a lady's lead
(Does the husband tax the Congo for the monkey's
  keep?)
The hopping monkey cannot follow the poodle
  dashing ahead.

Everyone holds his heart within his hands:

A prayer, a pledge of grace or gratitude
A devout offering to the god of summer, Sunday and
  plenitude.

The Sunday people are looking at hope itself.

They are looking at hope itself, under the sun, free from
  the teething anxiety, the gnawing nervousness
Which wastes so many days and years of
  consciousness.

The one who beholds them, beholding the gold and
        green
Of summer's Sunday is himself unseen. This is because
        he is
Dedicated radiance, supreme concentration, fanatically
        threading
The beads, needles and eyes – at once! – of vividness
        and permanence.
He is a saint of Sunday in the open air, a fanatic
        disciplined
By passion, courage, passion, skill, compassion, love:
        the love of life and the love of light as one, under
        the sun, with the love of life.

Everywhere radiance glows like a garden in stillness
        blossoming.

[Musée de l'Orangerie]
MONET'S "WATERLILIES"
for Bill and Sonja

Today as the news from Selma and Saigon
poisons the air like fallout,
    I come again to see
the serene great picture that I love.

Here space and time exist in light
the eye like the eye of faith believes.
    The seen, the known
dissolve in iridescence, become
illusive flesh of light
      that was not, was, forever is.

O light beheld as through refracting tears.
Here is the aura of that world
    each of us has lost.
Here is the shadow of its joy.

[Musée du Louvre]
RENOIR
for Donald Davie

Under striped flutter of awnings, they have come
together this afternoon to glitter with
carafes and wine glasses, and the fluffy dog
perched on the table amid parings
of apples and peaches. They rehearse
a civilization here among
bright collaborations of sun. The two
gentlemen nearest us take their ease
bare-armed, in undershirts. At the next
table, brown jacket and bowler melt
into ingenious dapple and nonchalance,
and only the farthest gentlemen, vertical, sustain
in suits and top hats, a dark
decorum. And ladies, ladies –
bonnetted, buttoned at neck
and wrists, yet ripe
with sleep: their cheeks
and half-closed eyes give them away.
Flesh is fruit, whispers the brush, and sunlight
wine; all cloth
dissolves. And when these chroma
and characters have faded
into the single, sensual blur of an afternoon

lost, there will remain
ghostly vermilion, hieroglyphic lips,
awning stripes and anemones that once
so vulgarly blazed, now dimming to
the mystic map of sprawl, spatter, and glare:
not Jeanne, Marie-Thérèse, Alphonse, Auguste,
    but this –
this truest pattern, radiance revealed,
a constellation visible at dusk.

FOR PROUST

Over and over something would remain
Unbalanced in the painful sum of things.
Past midnight you arose, rang for your things.
You had to go into the world again.

You stop for breath outside the lit hotel,
A thin spoon bitter stimulants will stir.
Jean takes your elbow, Jacques your coat. The stir
Spreads – you are known to all the personnel –

As through packed public rooms you press (impending
Palms, chandeliers, orchestras, more palms,
The fracas and the fragrance) until your palms
Are moist with fear that you will miss the friend

Conjured – but she is waiting: a child still
At first glance, hung with fringes, on the low
Ottoman. In a voice reproachful and low
She says she understands you have been ill.

And you, because your time is running out,
Laugh in denial and begin to phrase
Your questions. There had been a little phrase
She hummed, you could not sleep tonight without

Hearing again. Then, of that day she had sworn
To come, and did not, was evasive later,
Would she not speak the truth two decades later,
From loving-kindness learned if not inborn?

She treats you to a look you cherished, light,
Bold: "Mon ami, how did we get along
At all, those years?" But in her hair a long
White lock has made its truce with appetite.

And presently she rises. Though in pain
You let her leave – the loved one always leaves.
What of the little phrase? Its notes, like leaves
In the strong tea you have contrived to drain,

Strangely intensify what you must do.
Back where you came from, up the strait stair, past
All understanding, bearing the whole past,
Your eyes grown wide and dark, eyes of a Jew,

You make for one dim room without contour
And station yourself there, beyond the pale
Of cough or of gardenia, erect, pale.
What happened is becoming literature.

Feverish in time, if you suspend the task,
An old, old woman shuffling in to draw
Curtains, will read a line or two, withdraw.
The world will have put on a thin gold mask.

THÉÂTRE DE L'ODÉON

I could not rise from the dark and go out into the cool,
night air of that beautiful city,

could not get on with my conniving, young life.
What had been smooth and good became impossible,
    slowly,

mechanically, placing one foot in front of the next, so
    that legs,
as if buried in snow, might inch along the river

and the alleys with the clochards and the cats,
and I might seem a bright young thing again.

And all this before the shock of loss, the dying,
    who linger
with their weak bodies and blank faces,

and my own stupid share of human harm
inflicted upon the innocent,

and long before Time, that asp,
started laughing, *laughing* at me.

COUTURE

1.
Peony silks,
        in wax-light:
                that petal-sheen,

gold or apricot or rose
        candled into –
                what to call it,

lumina, aurora, aureole?
        About gowns,
                the Old Masters,

were they ever wrong?
        This penitent Magdalen's
                wrapped in a yellow

so voluptuous
        she seems to wear
                all she's renounced;

this boy angel
        isn't touching the ground,
                but his billow

of yardage refers
         not to heaven
                  but to pleasure's

textures, the tactile
         sheers and voiles
                  and tulles

which weren't made
         to adorn the soul.
                  Eternity's plainly nude;

the naked here and now
         longs for a little
                  dressing up. And though

they *seem* to prefer
         the invisible, every saint
                  in the gallery

flaunts an improbable
         tumble of drapery,
                  a nearly audible liquidity

(bright brass embroidery,
         satin's violin-sheen)
                  raveled around the body's

plain prose; exquisite
         (dis?)guises; poetry,
                  music, clothes.

2.
Nothing *needs* to be this lavish.
         Even the words I'd choose
                  for these leaves;

intricate, stippled, foxed,
         tortoise, mottled, splotched
                  —jeweled adjectives

for a forest by Fabergé,
         all cloisonné and enamel,
                  a yellow grove golden

in its gleaming couture,
         brass buttons
                  tumbling to the floor.

Who's it for?
         Who's the audience
                  for this bravura?

Maybe the world's
          just *trompe l'oeil*,
                    appearances laid out

to dazzle the eye;
          who could see through this
                    to any world beyond forms?

Maybe the costume's
          the whole show,
                    all of revelation

we'll be offered.
          So? Show me what's not
                    a world of appearances.

Autumn's a grand old drag
          in torched and tumbled chiffon
                    striking her weary pose.

Talk about your mellow
          fruitfulness! Smoky alto,
                    thou hast thy music,

too; unforgettable,
          those October damasks,
                    the dazzling kimono

worn, dishabille,
        uncountable curtain calls
                in these footlights'

dusky, flattering rose.
        The world's made fabulous
                by fabulous clothes.

FRENCH MOVIE

I was in a French movie
and had only nine hours to live
and I knew it
not because I planned to take my life
or swallowed a lethal but slow-working
potion meant for a juror
in a mob-related murder trial,
nor did I expect to be assassinated
like a chemical engineer mistaken
for someone important in Milan
or a Jew journalist kidnapped in Pakistan;
no, none of that; no grounds for
suspicion, no murderous plots
centering on me with cryptic phone
messages and clues like a scarf or
lipstick left in the front seat of a car;
and yet I knew I would die
by the end of that day
and I knew it with a dreadful certainty,
and when I walked in the street
and looked in the eyes of the woman
walking toward me I knew that
she knew it, too,
and though I had never seen her before,
I knew she would spend the rest of that day

with me, those nine hours walking,
searching, going into a bookstore in Rome,
smoking a Gitane, and walking,
walking in London, taking the train
to Oxford from Paddington or Cambridge
from Liverpool Street and walking
along the river and across the bridges,
walking, talking, until my nine hours
were up and the black-and-white movie
ended with the single word FIN
in big white letters on a bare black screen.

HOMAGE TO
THE POET

From TO VICTOR HUGO

O nursed in airs apart,
O poet highest of heart,
Hast thou seen time, who hast seen so many things?
   Are not the years more wise,
   More sad than keenest eyes,
The years with soundless feet and sounding wings?
   Passing we hear them not, but past
The clamour of them thrills us, and their blast.

   Thou art chief of us, and lord;
   Thy song is as a sword
Keen-edged and scented in the blade from flowers;
   Thou art lord and king; but we
   Lift younger eyes, and see
Less of high hope, less light on wandering hours;
   Hours that have borne men down so long,
Seen the right fail, and watched uplift the wrong.

   But thine imperial soul,
   As years and ruins roll
To the same end, and all things and all dreams
   With the same wreck and roar
   Drift on the dim same shore,
Still in the bitter foam and brackish streams
   Tracks the fresh water-spring to be
And sudden sweeter fountains in the sea.

ALGERNON CHARLES SWINBURNE (1837–1909)   201

MALLARMÉ'S TOMB

His sail should be his tomb, since no
Breath on this earth could convince
The skiff of his voice to say no
To the river's summons of light.

Here, he said, is Hugo's loveliest verse:
"The sun has set, this evening, in the clouds."
Water lets nothing be added or removed:
It turns to fire; by that fire he's consumed.

We see him blurring, far away, as his boat
Fades from view. At its prow, what is he
Waving? We can't tell – not from here.

Is that how people die? And who's he talking to?
What will be left of him, when night comes on?
Plowing the river, this two-colored scarf.

202 YVES BONNEFOY (1923–2016)
TRANSLATED BY HOYT ROGERS

TRISTE CORBIÈRE

A clamor of gulls
outside the French windows
above the tidepools
in the stone harbor
in Roscoff Brittany
in the Hôtel des Bains
top floor under the eaves
I look down and see
the damned poet
Tristan Corbière
walking along the quai
in this stone town
with its fishscale skies
where a street is named after him
a small dark stone street
twisting to the sea
Even at this distance
I see the black crow's feet
on his head
where a crow gripped him
and tried to fly away with him
Triste Corbière
with your countenance of night
Now a black gull
flies away with a fish

in the dark daylight
And a black crow watches
from a great height
an ebony crow
a huge crow
made of nothing but night
Only his feet are red
from holding the head of the poet
red with the blood of the poet
with his countenance of night

THE TOMB OF CHARLES BAUDELAIRE

Through the slimy open grating of a storm-drain
The entombed temple slobbers muck and rubies,
Abominable as the dog-god Anubis,
Whose muzzle blazes with a howl of savage pain.

It's like the new gas of an odorous campaign
Against the dark, illuminating our disease –
Immortal whore as old as Mephistopheles,
Who flits from lamp to lamp beside the foggy Seine.

What wreaths, in cities of no votive evenings,
Can offer benediction to us, as she flings
Herself in vain against a marble Baudelaire?

As trembling veils of light absent her from our gaze,
She has become his deadly-nightshade-poisoned air,
That we must breathe, although we perish in its maze.

STÉPHANE MALLARMÉ (1842–98)   205
TRANSLATED BY CIARAN CARSON

ANDRÉ BRETON

Like a grand piano with a horse's tail, with stars' trails
In the gloomy firmament
Heavy with coagulated blood
Whirling clouds, rainbows, phalanxes of planets, and
    myriads of birds
The indelible fire advances
The cypresses burn the tigers, the panthers, and the
    noble animals turn incandescent

Dawn's caution has been abandoned
And night hovers above the devastated earth

The treasure vault guards his name forever

MAX JACOB

Pray for the little acrobat with the yellow
cross, who envied a toad, pray

for him, an angel on days of defeat and
the cupbearer's laboratory animal

Cyprien there, Max here, clown who's bold
as an egg beneath his hat and weeps when bald

weeps blood and water all the Saviour's wounds
and then switches skins, black in Paris, white

in St-Benoît, a rainbow at Drancy
to celebrate the harlequin's mass

which opens Paradise. Pray for Max
king of Boeotia and prince of poets

who prayed so much for us, repeating that one breast
may stand in for another one, that beneath

the mask there's only one truth hidden
the same one: "We're going to die in a while."

GUY GOFFETTE (1947–)   207
TRANSLATED BY MARILYN HACKER

IN PARIS IN A LOUD DARK WINTER

In Paris in a loud dark winter

when the sun was something in Provence

when I came upon the poetry

of René Char

I saw Vaucluse again

in a summer of sauterelles

its fountains full of petals

and its river thrown down

through all the burnt places

of that almond world

and the fields full of silence

though the crickets sang

with their legs

And in the poet's plangent dream I saw

no Lorelei upon the Rhone

nor angels debarked at Marseilles

but couples going nude into the sad water

in the profound lasciviousness of spring

in an algebra of lyricism

which I am still deciphering

A BALLAD OF FRANÇOIS VILLON, PRINCE OF ALL BALLAD-MAKERS

Bird of the bitter bright grey golden morn
Scarce risen upon the dusk of dolorous years,
First of us all and sweetest singer born
Whose far shrill note the world of new men hears
Cleave the cold shuddering shade as twilight clears;
When song new-born put off the old world's attire
And felt its tune on her changed lips expire,
Writ foremost on the roll of them that came
Fresh girt for service of the latter lyre,
Villon, our sad bad glad mad brother's name!

Alas the joy, the sorrow, and the scorn,
That clothed thy life with hopes and sins and fears,
And gave thee stones for bread and tares for corn
And plume-plucked gaol-birds for thy starveling
     peers
Till death clipt close their flight with shameful shears;
Till shifts came short and loves were hard to hire,
When lilt of song nor twitch of twangling wire
Could buy thee bread or kisses; when light fame
Spurned like a ball and haled through brake and briar,
Villon, our sad bad glad mad brother's name!

Poor splendid wings so frayed and soiled and torn!
Poor kind wild eyes so dashed with light quick tears!
Poor perfect voice, most blithe when most forlorn,
That rings athwart the sea whence no man steers
Like joy-bells crossed with death-bells in our ears!
What far delight has cooled the fierce desire
That like some ravenous bird was strong to tire
On that frail flesh and soul consumed with flame,
But left more sweet than roses to respire,
Villon, our sad bad glad mad brother's name?

Envoi

Prince of sweet songs made out of tears and fire,
A harlot was thy nurse, a God thy sire;
Shame soiled thy song, and song assoiled thy shame.
But from thy feet now death has washed the mire,
Love reads out first at head of all our quire,
Villon, our sad bad glad mad brother's name.

VERLAINE'S TOMB

Where does it flow, this "shallow stream,"
If not in his verses? How well they know
That every shore is close, entangled
In the rushes of dream and desire.

When evening falls, words are judges:
Mud as much as light, they are truth.
This he never forgot – even when his phrases,
Grating, futile, lurched from rock to rock.

He was humble, and simple out of pride.
For others, he agreed to be a mirror, nothing more:
His silvering, pocked and worn, filters the sky.

Now they, in turn, must see that sky in him –
Deepening to red through darkened leaves,
When twilight shrouds the cooing of the doves.

YOU DID WELL TO LEAVE,
ARTHUR RIMBAUD!

You did well to leave, Arthur Rimbaud! Your eighteen years as obstinate about friendship, ill will and the silliness of Paris poets as about the buzzing of that pointless bee, your slightly mad Ardennes family, you did well to throw them to the winds, hurl them under the blade of their own precocious guillotine. You had reason to abandon the lazy boulevard, the bars with their lousy poems, for the beastly underworld, for wily commerce, the happiness of halfwits.

That absurd stride of body and spirit, that bullet that whacks its target, makes it burst, yes, that's really where it's at, the life of a man! After leaving childhood, one can't forever throttle one's brother. What if volcanos do change the place a little, and their lava, running through the world's great void, brings to it some qualities that sing among the wounds?

You did well to leave, Arthur Rimbaud! You got some of us wondering what luck we'd have if we did things your way.

RENÉ CHAR (1907–88)   213
TRANSLATED BY SUSANNE DUBROFF

PORTRAIT OF PAUL ÉLUARD

Dark teeth climb on the stars
What stars
A voice cries out on the lawn bruised
like a buttock
What buttocks
The wind covers the seeds' hair
The seeds will pass on
but your clouds will not
I have one in my pocket
which will rise clear up to my mouth
Then I'll smile at your stars

That's funny huh

214 BENJAMIN PÉRET (1899–1959)
TRANSLATED BY ELIZABETH R. JACKSON

DESNOS
regards to Bill Kulik

I considered the bourgeois virtues for one day
and it was my birthday when on a Wednesday
      morning
the palmist who walked among the corpses in
      Buchenwald
was sent on his journey by the Gestapo in Paris,
he, the dreamer of WXYZ,
he, the friend of Chico Marx and Bert Williams;
so much for thrift, hard work, piety and patriotism,
so much for not spending the principal and for the
      argument
against gratification and the argument for, and guess
how the light shone on my grandfather's stick and
      guess
what it was he carried in his dry mouth.

LITTLE ELEGY

Blaise Cendrars in his final days, old
and ill, wrote down his final words:
This morning on the windowsill a bird.
I find that so beautiful and moving
I can barely stand it, though
it makes me see the aged poet, head
turned toward the window and a small bird
perched there, staring in, angling its head
at the bulbous nose and squinty eyes:
I have come to visit you, old man.
But now I'll lift my wings and they will beat,
for flying is my great thrill,
and where the wings sprout out
is calling me to leap and fly.
Good-bye.
Morning, windowsill, and bird
all flown away. Good-bye, good-bye.

HOMAGE TO JEAN FOLLAIN

I think you must have written them on postcards, your
     poems, like something one sends home while
     visiting abroad;

or like woodcuts that one finds in an old book in the
     attic and stares at on a rainy day, forgetting
     supper, forgetting to switch on the light;

but not antique, though out of time, each fixed in its
     moment, like sycamore seeds spiralling down
     that never seem to reach the grass.

What became of the freak, the girl with animal fur,
     when the fair moved on to the next village?

and the old souse, when he got home from the
     wineshop, did he beat his wife or did she beat
     him? did his daughter run away?

and that horseman coming home from a thirty years
     war, did the dogs know him? why should that one
     bird cry to announce him from so far?

and the police, toiling day and night to manacle the
world, did they finish the last link, or did their
ink dry up? did their slide-rules crumble?

But you don't tell us, and perhaps you don't really
know, as you drink autumn wine in the evening,
leaning over the battlements of an imaginary
tower, watching the unwearied insects hovering
in the immaculate air.

THE DEATH OF GUILLAUME APOLLINAIRE

we know nothing
we knew nothing of grief
the bitter season of cold
carves long scars in our muscles
he would have sooner loved the joy of victory
wise with quiet sadnesses   caged
can do nothing

if snow fell upwards
if the sun rose here during the night
to warm us
and the trees hung with their wreath
– the only tear –
if the birds were among us to be reflected
in the quiet lake above our heads
ONE WOULD UNDERSTAND
death would be a fine long journey
and limitless holidays for flesh structures and bones

TRISTAN TZARA (1896–1963)   219
TRANSLATED BY LEE HARWOOD

REVOLUTION

From *THE PRELUDE*, BOOK 9

France lured me forth; the realm that I had crossed
So lately, journeying toward the snow-clad Alps.
But now, relinquishing the scrip and staff,
And all enjoyment which the summer sun
Sheds round the steps of those who meet the day
With motion constant as his own, I went
Prepared to sojourn in a pleasant town,
Washed by the current of the stately Loire.

Through Paris lay my readiest course, and there
Sojourning a few days, I visited
In haste, each spot of old or recent fame,
The latter chiefly, from the field of Mars
Down to the suburbs of St. Antony,
And from Mont Martre southward to the Dome
Of Genevieve. In both her clamorous Halls,
The National Synod and the Jacobins,
I saw the Revolutionary Power
Toss like a ship at anchor, rocked by storms;
The Arcades I traversed, in the Palace huge
Of Orleans; coasted round and round the line
Of Tavern, Brothel, Gaming-house, and Shop,
Great rendezvous of worst and best, the walk
Of all who had a purpose, or had not;
I stared and listened, with a stranger's ears,

To Hawkers and Haranguers, hubbub wild!
And hissing Factionists with ardent eyes,
In knots, or pairs, or single. Not a look
Hope takes, or Doubt or Fear is forced to wear,
But seemed there present; and I scanned them all,
Watched every gesture uncontrollable,
Of anger, and vexation, and despite,
All side by side, and struggling face to face,
With gaiety and dissolute idleness.

   Where silent zephyrs sported with the dust
Of the Bastille, I sate in the open sun,
And from the rubbish gathered up a stone,
And pocketed the relic, in the guise
Of an enthusiast; yet, in honest truth,
I looked for something that I could not find,
Affecting more emotion than I felt;
For 'tis most certain, that these various sights,
However potent their first shock, with me
Appeared to recompense the traveller's pains
Less than the painted Magdalene of Le Brun,
A beauty exquisitely wrought, with hair
Dishevelled, gleaming eyes, and rueful cheek
Pale and bedropped with overflowing tears.

From *THE YEAR OF HORRORS*

November 1870, i. On the Ramparts of Paris,
    at Nightfall

The east was black, although the west was bright –
As if some arm from Hades had been sent
To make a coffin porticoed with night
And drape two shrouds across the firmament.

And then the dark closed like a prison door.
Bird-cries and rippling plants were interknit.
I left. When I looked far away once more,
The sunset was a meager bleeding slit,

As if some duel had been contested by
A monster and a god of equal height,
And the appalling swordblade of the sky
Lay red across the ground after their fight.

VICTOR HUGO (1802–85)   225
TRANSLATED BY E. H. AND A. M. BLACKMORE

MARIE ANTOINETTE

The plate-glass windows gleam in the sun
    In the Tuileries Castle gaily;
And yet the well-known spectres of old
    Still walk about in it daily.

Queen Marie Antoinette still doth haunt
    The famous pavilion of Flora;
With strict etiquette she holds her court
    At each return of Aurora.

Full dress'd are the ladies, – they most of them stand,
    On tabourets others are sitting,
With dresses of satin and gold brocade,
    Hung with lace and jewels befitting.

Their waists are small, their hoop-petticoats swell,
    And from underneath them are peeping
Their high-heel'd feet, that so pretty appear, –
    If their heads were but still in their keeping!

Not one of the number a head has on,
    The queen herself in that article
Is wanting, and so Her Majesty boasts
    Of frizzling not one particle.

Yes, she with the toupée as high as a tower,
    In dignity so resplendent,
Maria Theresa's daughter fair,
    The German Caesar's descendant,

She, curlless and headless, now must walk
    Amongst her maids of honour,
Who, equally headless and void of curls,
    Are humbly waiting upon her.

All this from the French Revolution has sprung,
    And its doctrines so pernicious,
From Jean Jacques Rousseau and the guillotine,
    And Voltaire the malicious.

Yet strange though it be, I shrewdly think
    That none of these hapless creatures
Have ever observed how dead they are,
    How devoid of head and features.

The first *dame d'atour* a linen shift brings,
    And makes a reverence lowly;
The second hands it to the queen,
    And both retire then slowly.

The third and fourth ladies curtsy and kneel
    Before the queen discreetly,
That they may be able to draw on
    Her Majesty's stockings neatly.

A maid of honour curtsying brings
    Her Majesty's robe for the morning;
Another with curtsies her petticoat holds
    And assists at the queen's adorning.

The mistress of the robes with her fan
    Stands by, the time beguiling;
And as her head is unhappily gone,
    With her other end she is smiling.

LOUIS XVI GOES TO THE GUILLOTINE

Stink stink stink
What's that stink
It's Louis XVI that bad egg
and his head drops into the basket
his rotten head
since the cold is terrific this 21st of January
It rains blood it rains snow
and all sorts of other filth
that flourishes out of his ancient corpse
like a dog croaked on the bottom of a pail
in the midst of dirty laundry
who has had plenty of time to start decomposing
like the fleur-de-lys on the garbage can
which the cows refuse to nibble
for they give off an odor of true divinity
god the father of all mud
who gave to Louis XVI
the divine right to croak
like a dog in a laundry-pail

BENJAMIN PÉRET (1899–1959)   229
TRANSLATED BY CHARLES SIMIC

PARISIAN WAR CRY

Spring is at hand, for lo,
Within the city's garden plots
The government's harvest is beginning to grow –
But the gardeners call the shots!

O May! What bare-assed ecstasy!
Sèvres, Meudon, Bagneux, Asnières,
Hear our Farmer-Generals, busy
Planting in the empty air!

Guns and sabers glitter in parade,
Bright-mouthed weapons pointing straight ahead –
It's a treat for them to beat their feet
In the mud of a river running red!

Never, never now will we move back
From our barricades, our piles of stone;
Beneath their clubs our blond skulls crack
In a dawn that was meant for us alone.

Like Eros, politicians hover overhead,
Their shadows withering the flowers:
Their bombs and fires paint our garden red:
Their beetle-faced forces trample ours . . .

They are all great friends of the Grand Truc!
Their chief in his gladiolus bed blinks
Back his tears, puts on a sorrowful look,
Sniffs smoke-filled air, and winks.

The city's paving stones are hot
Despite the gasoline you shower,
And absolutely, now, right now, we've got
To find a way to break your power!

Bourgeois, bug-eyed on their balconies,
Shaking at the sound of breaking glass,
Can hear trees falling on the boulevards
And, far off, a shivering scarlet clash.

ARTHUR RIMBAUD (1854–91)
TRANSLATED BY PAUL SCHMIDT

WAR, OCCUPATION,
RESISTANCE

IN PARIS

On Victory Day when the soldiers come home …
Everyone will want to see THEM
The sun will open up early like a candy store on
      Valentine's Day
It'll be springtime in the Bois de Boulogne or out
      toward Meudon
All the cars will be perfumed and the poor horses will
      eat flowers
In the windows the little girls orphaned by the war
      will all have beautiful patriotic dresses
Photographers straddling the limbs of chestnut trees
      along the boulevards will aim their shutters
There'll be a circle around the movie cameraman
      who'll swallow up the historic procession better
      than a sword swallower
In the afternoon
The wounded will hang their Medals on the Arch of
      Triumph and go home without limping
Then
That evening
The place de l'Étoile will rise up into the sky
The dome of the Invalides will sing out over Paris like
      an immense golden bell

And the voices of a thousand newspapers will acclaim
    "La Marseillaise"
Woman of France

Paris, October 1916

236 BLAISE CENDRARS (1887–1961)
    TRANSLATED BY RON PADGETT

RAIN AND THE TYRANTS

I stand and watch the rain
Falling in pools which make
Our grave old planet shine;
The clear rain falling, just the same
As that which fell in Homer's time
And that which dropped in Villon's day
Falling on mother and on child
As on the passive backs of sheep;
Rain saying all it has to say
Again and yet again, and yet
Without the power to make less hard
The wooden heads of tyrants or
To soften their stone hearts,
And powerless to make them feel
Amazement as they ought;
A drizzling rain which falls
Across all Europe's map,
Wrapping all men alive
In the same moist envelope;
Despite the soldiers loading arms,
Despite the newspapers' alarms,
Despite all this, all that,
A shower of drizzling rain
Making the flags hang wet.

JULES SUPERVIELLE (1884–1960)   237
TRANSLATED BY DAVID GASCOYNE

RICHARD II FORTY

My country now is like a barge
Left by the haulers to the reef
And I am like that king in charge
Of more misfortune than belief
Still am I king of all my grief

For living now is just a dodge
For tears the wind's no handkerchief
In all I love my hate must lodge
What I have lost gives them relief
Still am I king of all my grief

The heart knows how to beat no more
The blood just stirs so cold and brief
Let two and two not add to four
When Grundy says fly like a thief
Still am I king of all my grief

Whether the sun should live or die
The colours wither from the leaf
Sweet Paris of my youth goodbye
And Quai-aux-Fleurs in spray and sheaf
Still am I king of all my grief

Desert the woods the fountains flee
You birds so quarrelsome be brief
Your songs are sent to Coventry
The bird-catcher reigns as chief
Still am I king of all my grief

There is a time to suffer pain
When Joan brought Vaucouleurs relief
Oh cut France into shreds again
The light was pallid on the leaf
Still am I king of all my grief*

* Written after the fall of France in World War II.

LOUIS ARAGON (1897–1982)

TRANSLATED BY PETER DALE

CURFEW

So what the door was guarded
So what we were imprisoned there
So what the street was barred off
So what the town was under attack
So what she was famished
So what we were without arms
So what night had fallen
So what we made love.

240 PAUL ÉLUARD (1895–1952)
TRANSLATED BY WILLIAM CARLOS WILLIAMS

RUE SAINT-MARTIN COUPLETS

I've gone off the Rue Saint-Martin
Since André Platane went away.
I've gone off the Rue Saint-Martin,
I've gone off wine, off everything.

I've gone off the Rue Saint-Martin
Since André Platane went away.
He was my friend, my mate.
We shared a room and a plate.
I've gone off the Rue Saint-Martin.

He was my friend, my mate.
He disappeared one day,
No one knows how or why, they took him away.
We never saw him again in the Rue Saint-Martin.

No point in imploring the saints,
Merri, Jacques, Gervais and Martin,
Not even Valérien tucked up on the hill.
Time goes by and still we know nothing.
André Platane has left the Rue Saint-Martin.

ROBERT DESNOS (1900–45)   241
TRANSLATED BY OLIVIA McCANNON

From *THE SONG OF THE DEAD*

Under the Harsh Wind

To appease the somersaults of famine
Here is the incandescent snow
The white bread
Stalk by stalk the ocean's sheaves line up
No more space or nourishment on earth
The ribbon of freedom
Head without brow bare heart without pride
Man surfeited with his lofty stature
Patience of nights of relentless days
He has his eyes lost in the openings
On the metal avenues
But the tired confessions saved from torture
Perfidious praise in the word's chiaroscuro
Under the jagged blade of an uncertain language
An abyss filled with little-known shames
Joy is harsh
Thought disperses at the current's breath
Tombs closed again
Treasure of the too weighty world

242 PIERRE REVERDY (1889–1960)
TRANSLATED BY MARY ANN CAWS

COURAGE

Paris is cold Paris is hungry
Paris no longer eats chestnuts in the streets
Paris has put on an old woman's old clothes
Paris sleeps standing airless in the Métro
More misery still is heaped upon the poor
And the wisdom and the folly
Of unhappy Paris
Are the fire and the pure air
Are the beauty and the goodness
Of her hungry toilers
Do not cry for help Paris
You are alive with a life without equal
And behind the bareness
Of your pallor and your thinness
All that is human is revealed in your eyes
Paris my handsome city
Sharp as a needle strong as a sword
Artless and erudite
You do not bear injustice
For you it is the only chaos
You will free yourself Paris
Paris twinkling like a star
Our surviving hope
You will free yourself from dirt and weariness
Brothers let us have courage

We who are not helmeted
Nor booted nor gloved nor well brought up
A ray lights up in our veins
Our light comes back to us
The best of us have died for us
And their blood now finds again our hearts
And it is morning once more a Paris morning
The dawn of deliverance
The space of spring new born
Senseless force has the worst of it
These slaves our enemies
If they have understood
If they are capable of understanding
Will rise up.

1942

244 PAUL ÉLUARD (1895–1952)
TRANSLATED BY GILBERT BOWEN

LIBERTY

On my schoolboy's copy-books
On my desk and on the trees
On sand and snow
I write your name

On all pages read
On all blank pages
Stone blood paper or ash
I write your name

On the gilded images
On the arms of warriors
On the crown of kings
I write your name

On the jungle and the desert
On nests on gorse
On the echo of my childhood
I write your name

On the wonders of the nights
On the white bread of the days
On seasons betrothed
I write your name

On all my rags of blue
On the pond musty sun
On the lake living moon
I write your name

On the fields on the horizon
On the wings of birds
And on the mill of shadows
I write your name

On every whiff of daybreak
On sea on ships
On the raging mountain
I write your name

On the foam of clouds
On the toil of storm
On the dense and tasteless rain
I write your name

On gleaming shapes
On bells of colour
On physical truth
I write your name

On awakened paths
On roads spread out

On overflowing squares
I write your name

On the lamp that kindles
On the lamp that dies
On my houses joined together
I write your name

On the fruit cut in two
By the mirror and my room
On my bed empty shell
I write your name

On my greedy loving dog
On his pricked up ears
On his awkward paw
I write your name

On the threshold of my door
On familiar things
On the surge of blessed fire
I write your name

On all accordant flesh
On the foreheads of my friends
On every hand held out
I write your name

On the window of surprises
On attentive lips
High above the silence
I write your name

On my devastated shelters
On my perished beacons
On the walls of my fatigue
I write your name

On absence without desire
On barren solitude
On the steps of death
I write your name

On health returned
On vanished risk
On hope without remembrance
I write your name

And by the power of a word
I begin my life again
I was born to know you
To name you

Liberty.

1942

248 PAUL ÉLUARD (1895–1952)
TRANSLATED BY GILBERT BOWEN

"THERE'S NO MORE WAR"

There's no more war. The ocean is distant. The wide river flowing through the city reflects domes and archways. Some people are already asleep on makeshift beds of rags and papers. It's the first day of winter. Motor cars drive through the swiftly fallen night. There are almost no more horses. Still, the clatter of horseshoes is a sound familiar enough not to surprise you. Nor does the jingle of bells on a collar, the masterwork of a harness-maker always up at the crack of dawn, in command of himself and yet subject to the anguishes of night.

JEAN FOLLAIN (1903–71)   249
TRANSLATED BY MARY FEENEY AND
WILLIAM MATTHEWS

ACKNOWLEDGMENTS

Thanks are due to the following copyright holders for permission to reprint:

GUILLAUME APOLLINAIRE: "Trip to Paris" by Guillaume Apollinaire, translated by Roger Shattuck, from *Selected Writings*, copyright © 1971 by Roger Shattuck. Reprinted by permission of New Directions Publishing Corp.; "Le Pont Mirabeau", translated by W. S. Merwin, from *The Anchor Anthology of French Poetry from Nerval to Valéry in English Translation* (ed. Angel Flores). Anchor Books, a division of Penguin Random House; excerpt from "Zone", translated by Beverley Bie Brahic, from *The Little Auto*. Reprinted with permission from CB Editions. LOUIS ARAGON: "Richard II Forty", translated by Peter Dale, from *Narrow Straits, Poems from the French*, Hippopotamus Press, 1985. Reprinted with permission from Hippopotamus Press. ANTONIN ARTAUD: "Verlaine Drinks", translated by Helen Weaver, from Antonin Artaud, *Selected Writings*, Farrar, Straus & Giroux. Georges Borchardt Agency. WILLIS BARNSTONE: "Has Paris Changed?" Reprinted with permission from the poet. CHARLES BAUDELAIRE: "Twilight: Daybreak" and "The Soul of the Wine" from *Les Fleurs du Mal* by Charles Baudelaire, translated by Richard Howard. Copyright © Richard Howard, 1982. Reprinted by permission of David R. Godine, Publisher; "Be Drunk", translated by Louis Simpson, from *Modern Poets of France: A Bilingual Anthology*, Story Line Press. The Estate of Louis Simpson. SAMUEL BECKETT: "Sanies II" from *Collected Poems of Samuel Beckett*, Grove Press, 2012, Faber & Faber, 2012. ELIZABETH BISHOP: "Sleeping on the Ceiling" from *Complete Poems 1927–1979*, Farrar, Straus & Giroux. YVES BONNEFOY: "Verlaine's Tomb" and "Mallarmé's Tomb", translated by Hoyt Rogers, from *Second Simplicity*, Yale University Press, 2011. Reproduced with permission of the Licensor through PLSclear. ANDRÉ BRETON: "The Free Union", translated by Samuel Beckett, *Collected Poems of Samuel Beckett*, Grove Press, 2012, Faber & Faber, 2012. CHARLES BUKOWSKI: "Paris" from *Betting on the Muse: Poems & Stories* by Charles Bukowski. Copyright © 1996 by Linda Lee Bukowski. Reprinted by permission of HarperCollins Publishers. GRACE CAVALIERI: "Hôtel Saint Germain". Reprinted with permission from the poet. BLAISE CENDRARS: "In Paris" and excerpt from "The Prose of the Trans-Siberian and of Little Jeanne of France" in *Complete Poems of Blaise Cendrars*, University of California Press, 1992. Translated by Ron Padgett. Reprinted with permission conveyed through Copyright Clearance Center, Inc. AIMÉ CÉSAIRE: "The Griffin", translated by Gregson Davis, from *Non-Vicious Circle*, Stanford University Press, 1984. RENÉ CHAR: "You Did Well to Leave, Arthur Rimbaud!", translated by Susanne Dubroff, from *The Smoke That Carried Us, Selected Poems*, White Pine Press, 2004. HENRI COLE: "Paris Is My Seroquel". Reprinted with permission from the poet. BILLY COLLINS: "January in Paris" from *Ballistics*, Random House, 2008. FRANÇOIS COPPÉE: "Paris", translated by

Kendall Lappin, from *Dead Poets Speak Plain English, An Anthology of Poems – French*, Asylum Arts Press, 1997; Leaping Dog Press, 2005. TRISTAN CORBIÈRE: "Paris at Night" from *The Anchor Anthology of French Poetry from Nerval to Valéry in English Translation* (ed. Angel Flores). Anchor Books, a division of Penguin Random House. GREGORY CORSO: Gregory Corso, "Paris" from *Gasoline & Vestal Lady on Brattle*. Copyright © 1955, 1958 by Gregory Corso. Reprinted with the permission of The Permissions Company, Inc., on behalf of City Lights Books, www.citylights.com. JULIO CORTÁZAR: Julio Cortázar, "Le Dôme", translated by Stephen Kessler, *Save the Twilight: Selected Poems*. Copyright © 1984 by Julio Cortázar and the Heirs of Julio Cortázar. English translation copyright © 1997 and 2016 by Stephen Kessler. Reprinted with the permission of The Permissions Company, Inc., on behalf of City Lights Books, www.citylights.com. BARBARA CROOKER: "Les Boulangers", from *Les Fauves*. Reprinted with permission from the poet. COUNTEE CULLEN: "At the Étoile" from *Collected Poems*. Copyright owned by Amistad Research Center, New Orleans, LA. Licensing administered by Thompson and Thompson. E. E. CUMMINGS: "Paris; this April sunset completely utters", from *Complete Poems*, Liveright Publishing Corporation, 1923. GÉRARD DE NERVAL: "A Path in the Luxembourg", translated by Olivia McCannon, from *Paris: poetry of place*, edited by Hetty Meyric-Hughes, published by Eland Publishing Limited, London, 2014. Reprinted by permission from the translator. EUSTACHE DESCHAMPS: "Paris is Beyond Compare" by Eustache Deschamps, translated by David Curzon and Jeffrey Fiskin. Republished with permission of Routledge Publishing, Inc., from *Eustache Deschamps: Selected Poems*, 2003; permission conveyed through Copyright Clearance Center, Inc. ROBERT DESNOS: "I Have Dreamed of You So Much", translated by Paul Auster, from *Collected Poems of Paul Auster*, Overlook Press, 2004." Rue Saint-Martin Couplets", translated by Olivia McCannon, first published in *Modern Poetry in Translation*, Series 3, No. 15; taken from *Paris*, published by Eland Publishing Limited, London, 2014. Reprinted by permission from the translator. MARK DOTY: "Couture" from *Atlantis* by Mark Doty. Copyright © 1995 by Mark Doty. Reprinted by permission of HarperCollins Publishers. RITA DOVE: "The Island Women of Paris" from *Grace Notes*, W.W. Norton, 1989. PAUL ÉLUARD: translated by William Carlos Williams: "Curfew" by William Carlos Williams, translated from the French of Paul Éluard, from *The Collected Poems: Volume II, 1939–1962*, copyright © 1948 by William Carlos Williams. Reprinted by permission of New Directions Publishing Corp. "Lady Love" translated by Samuel Beckett, *Collected Poems of Samuel Beckett*, Grove Press, 2012, Faber & Faber, 2012. "The Earth Is Blue Like an Orange", translated by Mary Ann Caws, from *The Yale Anthology of Twentieth-Century French Poetry*, Yale University Press, 2004. "Courage" and "Liberty", translated by Gilbert Bowen, from *Selected Poems, Paul Éluard*, Riverrun Press, 1987. JAMES A. EMANUEL: "Bojangles and Jo". Copyright © by James A. Emanuel. LÉON-PAUL

251

FARGUE: "At Saint-Germain", translated by Wallace Fowlie, from *Mid-Century French Poets*, Grove Press, 1955. JAMES FENTON: "In Paris with You" from *Yellow Tulips, Poems 1968–2011*, Faber & Faber, 2011, also from *Out of Danger, Selected Poems* (Farrar, Straus & Giroux, 2006). Reprinted with permission from Farrar, Straus & Giroux. Sterling Lord Literistic. LAWRENCE FERLINGHETTI: "Plan du Centre de Paris à Vol d'Oiseau", by Lawrence Ferlinghetti, from *European Poems and Transitions*, copyright © 1984 by Lawrence Ferlinghetti. "In Paris in a Loud Dark Winter" by Lawrence Ferlinghetti, from *These Are My Rivers*, copyright © 1955 by Lawrence Ferlinghetti. "Triste Corbière" by Lawrence Ferlinghetti, from *European Poems and Transitions*, copyright © 1980 by Lawrence Ferlinghetti. Reprinted by permission of New Directions Publishing Corp. ZELDA FITZGERALD: excerpt [102 words] from "Letter to F. Scott Fitzgerald" from *Zelda Fitzgerald, The Collected Writings*, Scribner, 1991. JEAN FOLLAIN: excerpt from "Streets", translated by Helen Constantine, in *Paris Street Tales* (Oxford University Press, 2016); "There's no more war", translated Mary Feeney and William Matthews, from *Dreaming the Miracle*, White Pine Press, 2003. EMILY FRAGOS: "Théâtre de l'Odéon". Reprinted with permission from the poet. JEAN GENET: excerpt from *A Song of Love*, translated by Steven Finch, from *Treasures of the Night, The Collected Poems of Jean Genet*, Gay Sunshine Press, 1981. GUY GOFFETTE: "Max Jacob" translated by Marilyn Hacker, from *The Yale Anthology of Twentieth-Century French Poetry*, Yale University Press, 2004. Reproduced with permission of the Licensor through PLSclear. MARILYN HACKER: "Rue des Écouffes" from *Desesperanto, Poems 1999–2002*, W. W. Norton & Company; translation by Marilyn Hacker of "Max Jacob" by Guy Goffette, from *Charlestown Blues*, University of Chicago Press, 2007. By permission of Frances Collin Agency, and the poet. ROBERT HAYDEN: "Monet's 'Waterlilies'", from *Collected Poems of Robert Hayden*, Liveright Publishing Co., 1990. ERNEST HEMINGWAY: "Montparnasse" from *Complete Poems*. The Ernest Hemingway Foundation. NAZIM HIKMET: "Before the time runs out, my rose" translated by Nilüfer Mizanoğlu Reddy. EDWARD HIRSCH: "Colette" from *On Love: Poems* by Edward Hirsch, copyright © 1998 by Edward Hirsch. Used by permission of Alfred A. Knopf, an imprint of the Knopf Doubleday Publishing Group, a division of Penguin Random House LLC. All rights reserved. LANGSTON HUGHES: "Montmartre" and "Jazz Band in a Parisian Cabaret" from *The Collected Poems of Langston Hughes* by Langston Hughes, edited by Arnold Rampersad with David Roessel, Associate Editor, copyright © 1994 by the Estate of Langston Hughes. Used by permission of Alfred A. Knopf, an imprint of the Knopf Doubleday Publishing Group, a division of Penguin Random House LLC. All rights reserved. "Montmartre" and "Jazz Band in a Parisian Cabaret" from *The Collected Poems of Langston Hughes* by Langston Hughes, Harold Ober Associates. VICTOR HUGO: excerpt from *The Year of Horrors*, "November 1870, On the Ramparts of Paris, at Nightfall", translated by E. H. and A. M.

Blackmore, from *Selected Poems of Victor Hugo*, University of Chicago Press, 2001. VICENTE HUIDOBRO: "Blind", translated by L. C. Breunig, from *The Cubist Poets in Paris, An Anthology*, University of Nebraska Press, 1995. MAX JACOB: "La Rue Ravignan", translated by William T. Kulik, from *Dreaming the Miracle, Three French Prose Poets: Jacob, Ponge, Follain*, White Pine Press, 2003. FADY JOUDAH: "Arc de Triomphe" from *Textu*. Copyright © 2014 by Fady Joudah. Reprinted with the permission of The Permissions Company, Inc. on behalf of Copper Canyon Press, www.coppercanyonpress.org. HÉDI KADDOUR: "The Bus Driver", translated by Marilyn Hacker, from *Treason* by Hédi Kaddour, Yale University Press, 2012. Reproduced with permission of the Licensor through PLSclear. VICTORIA KENNEFICK: "Paris Syndrome", originally published in *Poetry* magazine. Reprinted with permission from the poet. GALWAY KINNELL: "Les Invalides" from *Mortal Acts, Mortal Words* by Galway Kinnell. Copyright © 1990, renewed 2008 by Galway Kinnell. Reprinted by permission of Houghton Mifflin Harcourt Publishing Company. All rights reserved. DAVID KIRBY: "To a French Structuralist" by David Kirby from *A Book of Luminous Things, An International Anthology of Poetry*. Selection copyright © 1996 by Czeslaw Milosz. Reprinted by permission of Houghton Mifflin Harcourt Publishing Company. All rights reserved. KENNETH KOCH: "To the French Language" from *The Collected Poems of Kenneth Koch* by Kenneth Koch, copyright © 2005 by The Kenneth Koch Literary Estate. Used by permission of Alfred A. Knopf, an imprint of the Knopf Doubleday Publishing Group, a division of Penguin Random House LLC. All rights reserved. JULES LAFORGUE: "Spring Evening on the Boulevards", translated by William Jay Smith, from *The Anchor Anthology of French Poetry from Nerval to Valéry in English Translation* (ed. Angel Flores). Anchor Books, a division of Penguin Random House. DAVID LEHMAN: "French Movie" from *Yeshiva Boys*, Scribner, 2010. CLARENCE MAJOR: "No One Goes to Paris in August" from *Waiting for Sweet Betty*. Copyright © 2002 by Clarence Major. Reprinted with the permission of The Permissions Company, Inc., on behalf of Copper Canyon Press, www.coppercanyonpress.org. STÉPHANE MALLARMÉ: "O so dear from far away, so near and white", translated by Vernon Watkins, from *The Anchor Anthology of French Poetry from Nerval to Valéry in English Translation* (ed. Angel Flores). Anchor Books, a division of Penguin Random House. "The Tomb of Charles Baudelaire", translated by Ciaran Carson, taken from *Paris*, an anthology by Eland Publishing Limited, London, 2014. OSIP MANDELSTAM: "Notre Dame", translated by James Greene, from *Selected Poems of Osip Mandelshtam*, Penguin Books, 1989. JOYCE MANSOUR: "I Want to Sleep With You", translated by Mary Ann Caws, from *Surrealist Love Poems*, University of Chicago Press, 2002. PIERRE MARTORY: "Wine", translated by John Ashbery, from *The Landscapist* by Pierre Martory. Reprinted with permission from Sheep Meadow Press. Georges Borchardt Agency. JAMES MERRILL: "For Proust" from *Collected Poems* by James Merrill, copyright © 2001 by the Literary Estate of James

Merrill at Washington University. Used by permission of Alfred A. Knopf, an imprint of the Knopf Doubleday Publishing Group, a division of Penguin Random House LLC. All rights reserved. CZESLAW MILOSZ: "Bypassing Rue Descartes", translated by Renata Gorczynski and Robert Hass, from *New and Collected Poems 1931–2001*, Ecco Press. GABRIELA MISTRAL: "Rodin's Thinker", translated by Gustavo Alfaro, from *An Introduction to Literature*, 15th Edition, Pearson/Longman, 2008. CÉSAR MORO: "André Breton", translated by Willard Bohn, from *Surrealist Poetry, An Anthology*, Bloomsbury Academic, 2007. Reprinted with permission from Bloomsbury Publishing, Inc. STANLEY MOSS: excerpt from "Mon Père, Elegy for Paul Celan". Reprinted with permission from the poet. VLADIMIR NABOKOV: "The Paris Poem" from *Selected Poems* by Vladimir Nabokov, copyright © 2012 by The Estate of Vladimir Nabokov. Used by permission of Alfred A. Knopf, an imprint of the Knopf Doubleday Publishing Group, a division of Penguin Random House LLC. All rights reserved. The Wylie Agency. PABLO NERUDA: "Goodbye to Paris", translated by Alastair Reid, from *Extravagaria*, Farrar, Straus & Giroux, 1974. Reprinted with permission from Farrar, Straus & Giroux. Carmen Balcells Agency. HAROLD NORSE: "beat hotel, 9 rue gît-le-coeur" from *In the Hub of the Fiery Force: Collected Poems 1934–2003*, published by Thunder's Mouth Press. Copyright owned by The Regents of the Univeristy of California Press, Bancroft Library, UC Berkeley. Reprinted with permission. FRANK O'HARA: "For Poulenc" from *The Collected Poems of Frank O'Hara* by Frank O'Hara, copyright © 1971 by Maureen Granville-Smith, Administratrix of the Estate of Frank O'Hara, copyright renewed 1999 by Maureen O'Hara Granville-Smith and Donald Allen. Used by permission of Alfred A. Knopf, an imprint of the Knopf Doubleday Publishing Group, a division of Penguin Random House LLC. All rights reserved. RON PADGETT: "Little Elegy" and "Bastille Day" from *Collected Poems*. Copyright © 2002, 2007 by Ron Padgett. Reprinted with the permission of The Permissions Company, Inc. on behalf of Coffee House Press, www.coffeehousepress.com. BENJAMIN PERET: "Louis XVI Goes to the Guillotine", translated by Charles Simic, from *The Random House Book of Twentieth-Century French Poetry*, Random House (ed. Paul Auster), 1984. Vintage Books, a division of Penguin Random House. "Portrait of Paul Éluard", translated by Elizabeth R. Jackson, from *A Marvelous World*, LSU Press, 2013. MARIE PONSOT: "Rain All Night, Paris" from *Springing: New and Selected Poems* by Marie Ponsot, copyright © 2002 by Marie Ponsot. Used by permission of Alfred A. Knopf, an imprint of the Knopf Doubleday Publishing Group, a division of Penguin Random House LLC. All rights reserved. EZRA POUND: "In a Station of the Métro" by Ezra Pound, from *Personae*, copyright © 1926 by Ezra Pound. Reprinted by permission of New Directions Publishing Corp. Faber & Faber Limited. JACQUES PRÉVERT: "Place du Carrousel", translated by Lawrence Ferlinghetti, from *Paroles*. English translation copyright © 1958 by Lawrence Ferlinghetti. Reprinted with the permission of The

Permissions Company, Inc., on behalf of City Lights Books, www.citylights.com; "Paris at Night", "The Garden" and "Immense and Red", translated by Norman R. Shapiro, from *Préversities: A Jacques Prévert Sampler*, Black Widow Press, 2010. RAYMOND QUENEAU: "Cleanliness", translated by Rachel Galvin, from *Hitting the Streets*, Carcanet Press, 2013. PIERRE REVERDY: "Street Circus", translated by Ron Padgett, and excerpt from *The Song of the Dead*, "Under the Harsh Wind", translated by Mary Ann Caws, taken from *Pierre Reverdy*, edited by Mary Ann Caws, New York Review of Books, 2013. RAINER MARIA RILKE: "You don't know nights of love?", translated by Edward Snow, from *Uncollected Poems*, Farrar, Straus & Giroux, 1996. Reprinted with permission from Farrar, Straus & Giroux. ARTHUR RIMBAUD: "Parisian War Cry", from *Arthur Rimbaud: Complete Works*, translated from the French by Paul Schmidt. Copyright © 1967, 1970, 1971, 1972, 1975 by Paul Schmidt. Reprinted by permission of HarperCollins Publishers. MAURICE ROLLINAT: "The Mime", translated by Kendall Lappin, from *Dead French Poets Speak Plain English, An Anthology of Poems*, Asylum Arts Press, 1997; Leaping Dog Press, 2005. JACQUES ROUBAUD: "To the Eiffel Tower", "Dream of February 11, 19—", "Dream of August 17, 19—" and excerpt from "Arrondissements", translated by Keith and Rosemarie Waldrop, from *The form of a city changes faster, alas, than the human heart*, by Jacques Roubaud, Dalkey Archive Press, 2006. MARY JO SALTER: "Boulevard du Montparnasse" from *Sunday Skaters* by Mary Jo Salter, copyright © 1994 by Mary Jo Salter. Used by permission of Alfred A. Knopf, an imprint of the Knopf Doubleday Publishing Group, a division of Penguin Random House LLC. All rights reserved. DELMORE SCHWARTZ: excerpt from "Seurat's Sunday Afternoon Along the Seine" by Delmore Schwartz, from *Selected Poems*, copyright © 1959 by Delmore Schwartz. Reprinted by permission of New Directions Publishing Corp. Faber & Faber Limited. LÉOPOLD SÉDAR SENGHOR: "In Memoriam", by Leopold Sédar Senghor from *The Collected Poetry*, translated by Melvin Dixon, © 1991 by the Rector and Visitors of the University of Virginia. Reprinted by permission of the University of Virginia Press. PHILIPPE SOUPAULT "Horizon", translated by Rosemarie Waldop, from *The Random House Book of Twentieth-Century French Poetry* (ed. Paul Auster), 1984. Vintage Books, a division of Penguin Random House. JON STALLWORTHY: "Toulouse-Lautrec at the Moulin Rouge" from *Out of Bounds*, Oxford University Press, 1963. GERTRUDE STEIN: excerpt from "Hôtel François 1er" from *The Yale Gertrude Stein*, Yale University Press, 1980. Mr Stanford Gann, Jr., Levin & Gann, P. A., Literary Executor of the Estate of Gertrude Stein. GERALD STERN: "Desnos" from *Everything is Burning*, W. W. Norton, 2005. JULES SUPERVIELLE: "Rain and the Tyrants", translated by David Gascoyne, in *Collected Verse Translations* by David Gascoyne, Oxford University Press, 1970. WISLAWA SZYMBORSKA: "Clochard" and "Vocabulary" from *Map: Collected and Last Poems* by Wislawa Szymborska, translated from the Polish by Stanislaw Barańczak and Clare Cavanagh. English translation copyright © 2015 by Houghton Mifflin Harcourt Publishing Company. Reprinted by permission of Houghton Mifflin Harcourt Publishing Company. All rights reserved. JEAN TARDIEU: "The Seine in Paris", translated by David Kelley, from *The River Underground: Selected Poems and Prose* by Jean Tardieu, Bloodaxe Books, 1991. LUIS LÁZARO TIJERINA: "Chet Baker in Paris". Reprinted by permission of the poet. MARINA TSVETAEVA: "In Paris", translated by Sasha Dugdale, from *Paris*, Eland Publishing Limited, 2014. Reprinted with permission from the translator. GAEL TURNBULL: "Homage to Jean Follain" from *While breath persist*. Reprinted with permission from The Porcupine Quill, Ontario, and from *There are words: Collected Poems*, Shearsman Books, Exeter, 2006. Reprinted with permission from The Estate of Gael Turnbull. TRISTAN TZARA: "The great lament of my obscurity three", translated by William Rees, from *Penguin Book of French Poetry 1820–1950*, Penguin Books, 1990. "The Death of Guillaume Apollinaire", translated by Lee Harwood, from *The Selected Poems of Tristan Tzara*, Trigram Press, 1975. CÉSAR VALLEJO: "Black Stone Lying on a White Stone", translated by Robert Bly, from *Neruda and Vallejo, Selected Poems*, Beacon Press, 1971. MONA VAN DUYN: "At Père Lachaise" by Mona Van Duyn, copyright © 1982 by Mona Van Duyn; from *If It Be Not I: Collected Poems 1959–1982* by Mona Van Duyn. Used by permission of Alfred A. Knopf, an imprint of the Knopf Doubleday Publishing Group, a division of Penguin Random House LLC. All rights reserved. PAUL VERLAINE: "The Noise of the Cabarets", translated by Kate Flores, from *The Anchor Anthology of French Poetry from Nerval to Valéry in English Translation* (ed. Angel Flores), Anchor Books, a division of Penguin Random House. "Il Bacio", from *Poems Under Saturn/Poèmes saturniens* by Paul Verlaine, translated with an introduction by Karl Kirchwey. Copyright © 2011 by Princeton University Press. Reprinted with permission from Princeton University Press. ROSANNA WARREN: "Renoir" from *Each Leaf Shines Separate*, W. W. Norton, 1984. RICHARD WILBUR: [François Villon] "Ballade of Forgiveness" from *The Mind Reader* by Richard Wilbur. Copyright © 1971, and renewed 1999 by Richard Wilbur. Reprinted by permission of Houghton Mifflin Harcourt Publishing Company. All rights reserved. JAMES WRIGHT: "A First Day in Paris" from *Above the River: Complete Poems*. Noonday Press, Farrar, Straus & Giroux, 1992. Reprinted with permission from Farrar, Straus & Giroux. RICHARD WRIGHT: excerpt from *Haiku, This Other World*, Arcade Publishing, 1998. ADAM ZAGAJEWSKI: "Square d'Orléans" from *Without End, New and Selected Poems*. Reprinted with permission from Farrar, Straus & Giroux. Faber & Faber Limited.

Although every effort has been made to trace and contact copyright holders, in a few instances this has not been possible. If notified, the publishers will be pleased to rectify any omission in future editions.